WHO O
SPARSHOLT

A TOWNIE'S GUIDE TO WHAT'S HAPPENING ON THE LAND

Edmund Bush

ISBN 978-0-9558387-4-3

Printed and Published by
Sarsen Press
22 Hyde Street
Winchester SO23 7DR

Who Owns Sparsholt

A townie's guide to what's happening on the land

Foreword

My own experience of being a townie, commencing in Berlin and moving on to London via Vienna, later incorporating Toronto, Worcester (USA) and Stuttgart, enables me to put myself in a townie's shoes even though I have now been a country dweller for many years. It was my townie phase which imbued me with an ongoing hobby of walking in the countryside, and this has stayed with me even though I now live in it.

During my many years of walking 'on the land' I had often wondered about the people who owned it, and why there appeared to be some reservations on their part in allowing us townies on to their patch. With the 'definitive rights of way' clearly shown on our maps, the townies can at least be clear about where they can legitimately go, but many, including myself, think that even with the advent of the 'freedom to roam', our access is unnecessarily limited.

The experience which was seminal to my reaching for the pen, or more accurately the word processor, both, I like to believe, more powerful than the sword, occurred not far from where I live. I had uncovered what I saw as a historical right of way in the parish adjacent to Sparsholt, and one I considered to have been the continuation of a path shown as a cul-de-sac terminating at the parish boundary. I had established that a part of this continuation in the adjoining parish was marked on the older ordnance survey maps as 'The Drove', and duly filed a claim for it to be made a public right of way, partly and in addition based on evidence pertaining to the Yew trees lining the route in question, which is just over a mile long.

On the day before the public hearing, I ventured out along this route, now a farm track, to gather further evidence for this. After negotiating a barbed wire fence, and nervously aware that I was no longer on a definitive right of way, I eventually emerged from the cover of a small wood, and found myself on a bare grassy slope down to the distant farm. I then heard the sound of a claxon, followed by that of a car engine revving up. Whether the claxon was an alarm set off by some astral foreign body scanner or fulfilling a more mundane function not associated with my presence I have never established. Suffice to say I then saw a speck at the bottom of the hill heading in my direction, relentlessly growing larger and more ominous.

It all reminded me of the scene in the film 'Lawrence of Arabia', where the hero witnesses a similar apparition approaching through the desert heat haze for an unimaginable length of time, finally materialising in the towering form of Omar Sharif as an Arab sheik on a camel.

In my version, it turned out to be the farm manager in his Land Rover. He also towered, since I am only 5'6", and the running board of his vehicle appeared to be not far short of that. He addressed me in the time-honoured phrase I had become accustomed to over years of losing my way – "And what might you be doing here?" But he also added 'Sir', which presented a novel and rather flattering version.

Slightly flustered by this form of address, I explained the purpose and urgency of my mission (the hearing being scheduled for the following day), whereupon he enquired whether I had permission for this intrusion from the landowner. I confessed that I had not. As a consequence, he invited me to leave his land either by the route I had come upon, or the quickest possible alternative. Before I had time to pull myself up to my full 5'6" and ask to see his credentials, he drove off leaving me standing in a cloud of dust.

Little did he know I had already had prior contact with the landowner with a view to persuading him to donate the right of way in question, with the possibility of having it named after him in perpetuity, or longer if necessary. He had declined, not, I should add, to my total surprise, asking me instead how I would like to have multitudes trampling through my factory, which is how he saw his land. As a result of this conversation, I had felt that asking permission for my trespass, bearing in mind its purpose, would have been both embarrassing and ridiculous.

In the event, both the County Council, and after going to appeal, the Government Inspector, chose to dismiss the claim. This was of course a considerable disappointment both to me and others who had supported the claim. It did, however, finally convince me that something had to be done. Why, after ten centuries of putting up with the results of landownership conferred by William the Conqueror, or even his predecessors, are we denied the pleasure of walking across 'our' land along footpaths and farm lanes without creating any obstruction or inconvenience to the owners, or even only their tenants? Has the time finally arrived when we should regard the land as a common good, available to those who want to use it to make a living on the basis that they are tenants on the land owned by 'us'? (Or should that be 'the Crown'? Or maybe both? More of that later).

For a start, I felt it was time for me to find out who the landowners were, at least in my own Parish of Sparsholt, what they did with their land and why they, the private and sometimes even the public, landowners and their tenants are so intent on keeping the rest of us off it. This enterprise quickly span out of control, and what I had anticipated to be a spare time diversion turned out to be a full time occupation. At this stage, and based on the consideration that Sparsholt is a fairly representative parish in terms of proportions of public, private, arable, forestry and grazing land, the idea of a book about what's happening on the land in general germinated, treating Sparsholt as a microcosm in assessing the situation nationwide.

This in turn expanded further still after I reflected that what the landowners were doing with the land had significant effects not only for those living on it, or even the whole nation, but also the rest of our planet. So while I was looking at major landowners in the parish, why not include all landowners or even just tenants who were doing something of social import on the land they occupy?

Although this book is not intended to be a learned treatise, it is based on factual information rather than opinion or hearsay, at least wherever possible. To this end I have used material from other more learned works, together with information gathered from the internet based on reliable sources, many of them either government agencies or well known public bodies. Where significant, I have supplied the sources by way of numbered references in the appendix.

Finding out what was going on was in itself a major enterprise, and I hope that the fruits of my own hard earned and sometimes bitter experiences described will stimulate readers who are also townies living in the countryside to carry out researches into landownership, heritage and access in their own parishes.

With respect to landholding areas, and without wishing to offend those of a more traditional bent of mind, these are mainly given in hectares, abbreviated as 'ha'. The reason for this is not only an inborn propensity to question tradition, but also because all Ordnance Survey maps carry gridlines spaced in kilometres, which on the basis of 100ha to the square kilometre makes estimating landholding areas a doddle. Furthermore, it will keep readers after 2010 in step with what will by then be the only officially recognised units of land measurement. For those who still prefer to think in acres, I have added these in brackets where I felt it was important enough, but where I have failed to do so this can be arrived at approximately by multiplying the number of hectares by 2.5.

The landowners I looked at had holdings ranging in size from over 200ha down to 0.1ha, the qualifying condition being that its occupant did something of social significance with the land he, she or it (in the case of public institutions and trusts) occupied. The Parish was taken to be the land defined by the Boundary Commission. Although one would think this to be an obvious and widely published piece of information, the Parish boundaries can only be accessed by reference to the current Ordnance Survey map. This may also be firmed up with a copy of one's annual Council Tax demand to eliminate any uncertainty as regards one's parish affiliation.

The public understanding of 'landownership', meaning the state of being a landowner, is obvious to all of us. Nevertheless, in view of the importance of the term in the context of this book, I felt obliged to seek a legal definition of it. As a result, I feel I am no longer able to make a definitive statement about its meaning without a host of qualifying factors.

The reason for this is that the legality of landownership has developed from an original concept coined many centuries ago under what is known as common law, which informs us simply that 'The Crown is the only absolute owner of land in England and Wales'. Taking this statement at its face value would have resulted in a slender volume, with my rhetorical question 'Who owns Sparsholt' being answered by 'the Queen, of course, stupid!' Before you rush to take another close look at the deeds of your property, let me assure you that this simple statement does not imply the Crown has any immediate plans for asserting its rights to your land. It merely means that as with all English Law, which is based on the principle of 'case law', i.e. each case being judged by referring back to the judgement on a previous similar case, you will need a solicitor who can make a good living out of this system by pretending to make sense of it.

He, or she, will tell you that, as freeholders, we 'hold land of the Crown in free and common socage (feudal tenure of land involving payment of rent or other service to a superior)'. If you think this definition is a bit obfuscating, try this one which simply defines land as: 'If one be seized of some lands in fee, and possessed of other lands for years, all in one parish, and he grant all his lands in that (without naming them) in fee simple or for life; by this grant shall pass no, more but the land he hath in fee simple' (1). Please be aware that the quaint punctuation and grammar is not my typographical error.

In view of the above, you will breathe a sigh of relief if I say right away that I will not engage in a more detailed dissertation on the meaning or interpretation of landownership beyond assuring you that if you own the freehold of your property, you are (relatively) safe in assuming that you own the land and (in general) all the buildings erected on it. Furthermore, you are entitled to sell or pass it on to anyone you choose, in perpetuity.

Having got this far, I now have to confess to adding my own little obfuscation by using the term 'landowner' in this book to also encompass leaseholders whose lease has a minimum of seven years to run, since they will be responsible for what is happening on their land during their tenure.

It would have been interesting to find out if and where the crown has exercised its feudal right to landownership in recent times, but this would have extended the scope of this book beyond its primary purpose in addition to involving another year or so of research for which I had neither the time nor the inclination. For what it is worth, current legal opinion holds that the idea of the Queen demanding 'socage' is merely notional. It may be of interest to note, however, that all one's assets, including land, may become the property of the crown in certain circumstances, such as unclaimed or intestate assets including land of individuals or companies. These automatically revert to the Duchy of Cornwall on condition that this body uses them for the benefit of the public. And who is {or are} the Duchy of Cornwall? Good question, that.

As usual the internet has a ready answer: it's an estate created by Edward III for his son, and his successors, with the primary function of producing an income for the Prince of Wales, and his successors in title, to enable them to live in the style they have no doubt become accustomed to. Since the estate consists of over 57,000 ha spread over 23 counties, the Prince is obviously not short of pocket money.

In theory, and according to common law, a landowner can do what he likes with his land, and everything under it down to the centre of the earth and above it up to the heavens. Whether this entails an eventual guarantee of residence in the latter is not spelled out, but in any event the lofty simplicity of this concept of ownership has been spoiled by countless amendments in legislation enacted over the centuries. Amongst other tedious limitations, we cannot mine coal in our back garden, or prevent aeroplanes from flying through our piece of airspace. Another limitation is the law on treasure trove, which holds that any metal item found on the land which is more than 300 years old, or indeed any item more than 200 years old considered by the Secretary of State to be of outstanding historical, archaeological or cultural importance, automatically reverts to the Crown. There is, however, a code of practice for establishing suitable rewards for the finder as an inducement, perhaps, for owning up, basically to the extent of the value of the find as assessed by an independent panel set up by the government.

Since this book is aimed at those like myself who have no direct connection with the land beyond possibly owning the plot their dwelling occupies, I make no apologies for elaborating on matters which those who work on the land may consider obvious. The methods employed in obtaining my information are described in detail and should provide readers inclined on embarking on a similar quest in their own parishes with what I hope will prove to be invaluable assistance, if only by illustrating the many pratfalls open to them. A major resource in finding out who they (i.e. the landowners) are was the Land Registry, although it will become evident that local hearsay was an essential additional source. What the landowners do with their land, and why, was gleaned from interviews with landowners, farmers and/or their representatives and agents, and others whose activities on the land they occupy are of special interest to the parishioners. Not all the major landowners were accounted for, and the reasons for this were two-fold, either:

a) I was unable to trace the owners, or
b) the owners declined to be interviewed.

What the landowners, tenants and /or squatters (i.e. wildlife) are doing with the land may be patently obvious, but the long-term effects of their activities are not. This is of course the reason why these activities are increasingly regulated for environmental or other reasons of national interest, as are those connected with public access. Some of the landowners or their agents interviewed have made comments about these regulations. Where these, or indeed any comments not of a factual nature, are attributed to specific persons, they were submitted to them for approval prior to publication, as were those of non-landowning parishioners. Any other material not of a factual nature represents the author's views only and should not be attributed to any of the persons interviewed, for whose collaboration the author now wishes to express his appreciation, and who were:

Richard Monk, landowner/manager, Rookley Farm Ltd., Up Somborne, Hants

Philip Meitner, landowner/farmer, Moorcourt Farm, Sparsholt, Hants

Andrew Osmond, manager, Moorcourt Farm

Nicholas Craig Harvey, landowner/director, Lainston Estates, Sparsholt, Hants

Derek and Caroline Taylor, proprietors, Kirton Farm Nurseries Ltd., Sparsholt

Cliff Hasler, manager, Lainston House Hotel, Sparsholt

Valery Barnes, Lainston House Hotel retainer, Sparsholt

Norris Fuller, ex-manager, Church Farm, Sparsholt

Stephen Young, Head Teacher, Sparsholt Church of England Primary School

The Revd. Juliet Montague, Vicar of Sparsholt and the Downs Benefice

Peter May, ex Church Warden and Parochial Church Council member, St Stephen's Church, Sparsholt

Marie Bush, Secretary, Sparsholt Memorial Hall

Wendy Dean and Liz West, Sparsholt Playground Association

Terry and Jane Dunn, Ham Green Common Volunteers

John Steel, ex parish and city councillor

Alan Marlow, Ramblers' Association Access Officer for Hampshire

Linda Scorey, postmistress, The Well House Store

A considerable part of the Parish is publicly owned by Hampshire County Council, the Forestry Commission and Sparsholt College respectively. The representatives from these bodies who provided useful information were:

David Ball, Site Manager, Farley Mount Country Park,
    Hampshire County Council.
Tim Jackson, Principal, Sparsholt College
Graham Boyt, Farm Manager, Sparsholt College
Nick Hazlitt, Area Manager, West Hampshire Forestry
    Commission.

Information on muntjac deer was provided by Charles Smith-Jones, author of 'Muntjac – Managing an Alien Species', together with a sample muntjac steak which proved to be very tasty!

Other sources of information consulted were: the Land Registry, the Forestry Commission, Hampshire County Council, Sparsholt College, DEFRA (the Department for Environment, Food and Rural Affairs), the Dean and Chapter of Winchester and the Church Commissioners. Thanks are also due to the librarian at Lambeth Palace Library and the invariably helpful librarians at Winchester Reference Library (now at Winchester Discovery Centre).

Finally, my thanks to my wife Marie whose critical comments made me cautious of straying too far into unknown territory, and my friend Stephen Greenhalgh who cast his professional reader's eye over the draft and suggested many essential corrections and improvements. He also noticed my tendency to explore avenues not too closely associated with the topic in hand. These deviations I have refused to abandon since I believe that the reader will also find them interesting.

Contents

Illustrations

Introduction

By birth and upbringing a townie, I nevertheless managed to live most of my adult life adjacent to a field. This was no mere accident but a matter of choice, partly an escape from the high density living of my formative years coupled with a love of the countryside fostered by numerous holidays away from the madding crowd. Inevitably, I learnt from early on that there was a significant schism between those who happened to live next to the land and those who lived on it and made their living from it, or simply regarded it as a necessary appendage to their place of residence.

This may largely be due to a natural divergence of interests, which results in landowners and/or farmers, farm managers and farm workers tending to move in their own cliques with little interchange with the non-land based parishioners. A further barrier, not particularly applicable to Sparsholt, is due to the fact that where significant land areas are involved, the land owners are either aristocrats or at least belong with the upper classes due to their inherent wealth. The 'us' and 'them' situation is nevertheless still made amply clear once we (and I shall use this pronoun throughout this book as pertaining to the general public who individually own little more land than their home stands on), venture out on to the land. This aspect is dealt with in Part 7 under the heading 'Access'.

When it comes to 'public' land, i.e. land that in theory at least belongs to 'us', one might well suppose that the question of a 'schism' between 'us' and 'them' cannot exist. In fact, although in this case there cannot be a significant divergence of interests, due to the inevitably bureaucratic structures of the authorities involved, their response to their customers, or more correctly their employers, is not always what one would expect, as I will demonstrate anon.

As it happens, Sparsholt is representative of many parishes in England, be it Little Munching or Much Binding or even Over Culling (all, I hope, fictitious names), and for this reason the researches on which this book is based will, I fondly believe, prove to be of wider interest. In describing what is happening on the land in Sparsholt, and comparing this with what is happening on the land in general, my principal aim is to stimulate readers to take an interest in what is happening on a major national asset which will have far-reaching consequences for the future of all of us.

Being situated close to the city of Winchester, and within the Winchester district with a total population of 110,000[1], Sparsholt cannot claim to be either remote or isolated, nor can it boast of harbouring any (well let's say many) of the stereotype rural characters as portrayed on radio by The Archers and on TV by The Vicar of Dibley. It also exhibits certain traits not present in remoter rural parishes, the most important of these being the fact that a greater percentage of the inhabitants commute to a place of work which has little if any connection with the land. Nevertheless, with an ever growing number of commuters and increasing distances travelled by them, this difference is getting less marked by the day.

With a population of around 1000, of which a quarter are students at Sparsholt College, it falls within the umbrella definition of a rural community adopted by the National Statistics Office, as being a settlement of less than 10,000 inhabitants. This also tells us that one in five of the population of England and Wales live in a rural community, so what happens in Sparsholt could be said to be fairly representative for up to one fifth of Britain's population.

These figures do not touch on housing density, which would of course show up substantial differences within the rural communities. The inhabitants of Sparsholt are privileged in as far that all of them, even those whose homes may not incorporate much more land than the area taken up by the building, live no more than a few minutes walk from fields, woods and hedgerows.

What, and for that matter where, is Sparsholt? Just a parish to the West of Winchester in Hampshire, situated in the midst of fields, woodland and a country park, yet close enough to the city of Winchester to be incorporated within its district boundary, which extends to 160km (100 miles) and encompasses a total area of just over 640 square km (250 square miles). A parish where what is happening on the land has a direct effect on those who live there, even though only a minute proportion work 'on it', with most employed residents commuting to work in the larger conurbations of nearby Winchester, Southampton, Eastleigh, Basingstoke, Portsmouth and even London.

Historically, the boundary of the parish has remained unchanged over the last couple of hundred years, and encompasses 1486 ha (3672 acres). The term 'parish' has its origins in common law and Church of England divisions, but over time has become used for purposes of civil administration (hence 'civil' parish, to give it its full name). It is administered by an elected body, i.e. the parish council, and funded by an amount added on to the Council Tax by Hampshire County Council. The primary brief of the Parish Council is to promote the welfare of its parishioners by looking after local facilities such as bus shelters, parks, playgrounds, public seats, street lighting, leisure and recreation facilities, footpaths, cemeteries and village greens, traffic calming measures and the giving of grants to local voluntary organisations.

The name Sparsholt has a number of likely derivations, such as 'sparse wood' (Gaelic), 'chalk-stone wood' or 'spar or spear wood' from the timber which could be used for either (Anglo Saxon). The southern boundary of Sparsholt is formed by the Roman road from Winchester to Sarum which runs not far to the south of the site of the Sparsholt Roman Villa, whose mosaic floor is one of the permanent exhibits of the Winchester museum. Older still, and closer to this road, lie two large barrows which together with the mound at Farley Mount (a local landmark just outside the Parish boundary) and a group of smaller barrows nearby are proof of extensive ancient habitation in this area.

Having been a commuter for many years, I was fortunate in having a number of options as to where I chose to live. My attachment to the English countryside had been nurtured from the time I left London by the fact that subsequent homes in Buckinghamshire, Dorset and now Hampshire, have always been adjacent to open country. Since coming to Sparsholt I have become increasingly aware of the significance of the connection between landownership and my (and our) environment. This was partly due to the changes in our countryside which we have all witnessed. New developments have obliterated green spaces, hedgerows have disappeared and with them some of the associated wildlife, even the predominant seasonal colours of our landscape have changed quite dramatically from shades of green to the strident yellow of rape, the blue of hemp and more recently (in Sparsholt, anyway) the white of poppies. This illustrates how the activities of owners of the land, or their agents, and the farming community, have a profound effect on our environment.

Smaller occupiers of land also impact on our environment, sometimes more so than the big landowners. The post office and shop, the local playground, the village hall, the hotel, the pubs, the church and the school, are just some that play a significant part in our lives. When it comes to Public Landowners, a whole set of different forces are at work shaping our environment. Primarily, quite apart from financial considerations (largely determined by their budgets), their principal purposes are defined by Mission Statements laid down by government or county councils.

In accordance with my self-imposed brief, I have identified all the owners or long-term leaseholders, as the case may be, and examined the effect of their activities on the land and on us. The quest to find out who 'they' are has not been easy. Nor, for that matter, has it met with universal approval. To the contrary, in fact, since most of the people I informed about my mission took the view that I was poking my nose into other people's business. And why should I? How would I like it if some stranger approached me to find out what I was doing with my garden?

In my case, as a matter of fact, I have to confess that I would be quite flattered that anybody should care. What an opportunity to share all my gardening problems. The moss, the weeds, the never-ending hedge trimming, the permanent vigilance required to prevent my wife from pruning everything down to its roots, etc., etc. In fact, my inquisitor's eyes would have glazed over well before I had unloaded even half of my nascent landownership problems. Far from the nosy parker being rebuffed, he might quickly have come to regret his inquisitiveness.

Wanting to know about other people's business may therefore be an innate characteristic developed by me in the hope that eventually someone might be encouraged to try to find out about mine, to give me an opportunity to tell them at length, something life has denied me to date. Disraeli has been quoted as saying, 'Talk to a man about himself and he will listen for hours.' This has never happened to me, and I can't help thinking Disraeli must have been a very forbearing man. What he surely should have said is, 'never let a man go on about himself without interrupting unless you're prepared to listen for hours.' It has to be said that the negative reaction to this inquisitiveness of mine about others' business by friends and foes alike has prompted me to seriously question myself.

To illustrate the matter further, as part of my quest to find out who one of the local landowners was, I approached a land agent on the matter. Whilst on the subject, I should add that even tracking down the agent was not a task to be undertaken lightly, since the only source in this instance, anyway, was hearsay. My detective work paid off, however, and the agent in question instantly admitted full responsibility. He was also helpful to the extent of providing me with a detailed map showing all the land owned by his client who (or which?) happened to be a trust.

As part of my self-imposed brief to interview the landowners, I enquired about the address of the trust, only to be told by the agent that this information was confidential and he was not in a position to divulge it. I was (secretly) indignant at this, but remained composed, partly buoyed up by my conviction that if it was a trust, it would be registered as such and I would thereby be able to hunt down my prey anyway. But lo and behold, further researches at the local Reference Library and even the Internet found no address.

I then button-holed a local solicitor and challenged him to tell me how to locate the trust. He observed, coolly, I should add, that a trust was a private body such as any private individual, and why should any Tom, Dick or Harry need to know who they are and why. 'But', I said defensively, 'I am not any Tom, Dick or Harry'. 'Well, you might be as far as they are concerned. You might be soliciting a free hand-out, or snooping for confidential information. As it happens, you should know that this trust, through its local agent has, out of the kindness of its (collective?) heart, leased a piece of land at a peppercorn rent to the local school for recreational purposes'.

This gave me a chance to get in a quick repartee: 'Exactly so. And this is the sort of thing I want to put into my book. But how can I, if I don't know who they are and where they are'. Unmoved, my source was unable to throw further light on my conundrum.

Beaten and slightly bowed, I retired from further enquiries to reflect. There certainly appeared to be a widespread reluctance to accept my mission as worthwhile. Should I really press on to find out more about other people's business? Was this quest really based on a flaw in my character? Perhaps it was time I went to see a psychiatrist. After all, even my wife is concerned about me telling others about my business, and that's just people who have no interest in it.

After a period of depression, I was revived by an article in the press about the Land Registry which stated that this organisation not only registers all land transactions (with the qualifying condition of whereabouts in the country you live), but also reveals the amount of money involved in these transactions. Even in my wildest dreams, I would not have had the temerity to ask such a personal question. Furthermore, this organisation is financed by the taxpayer and employs thousands of people nationwide. Ergo, my curiosity can't be that strange after all!

It was a case of all hands back on deck. Mission: find out who owns the land, what they are doing with it, and why, and where we can have a say.

Part 1

Finding out

Before embarking on an account of my experiences connected with finding out who owns Sparsholt, and perhaps in the nature of an *hors d'oeuvre*, a cursory look at who used to own Sparsholt will help to put the remainder of the book in perspective.

1.1 Who used to own Sparsholt

Historically, landownership became of importance with the rise of 'the State', or in earlier times the Monarchy and the Church. All these institutions have wielded great authority over the land, and there was a time, not even a millennium ago, when all the land belonged to either the Monarch or the Church, or to those they had granted rights thereto. The Domesday Book, one of the earliest records of landownership in England, shows that the King and his family owned 17%, the Bishops and abbots 26%, and the 190 principal tenants 54%.[1]

In the case of the Crown, these would have been the aristocracy and powerful Barons who paid homage to it. They in turn would grant rights of tenure or use of their land to the lower gentry, who in turn let it to the peasants who actually did the hard work of gleaning the products from the soil, and these might also have employed lower castes such as serfs or slaves to assist them.

In the case of the Church, the land would have belonged to the Bishops, who in turn could grant tenure to lesser churchmen down to the level of monks. These in turn would either till the soil themselves, or leave this to the peasants. The earliest record of land tenure relating to the Church in Sparsholt relates to a grant by the first Christian Kings of Wessex Cynegils and his son Cynewalth of the Manor of Chilcomb, which included Sparsholt, to the Benedictine Abbot of Winchester in 639.

The earliest recorded landowners in Sparsholt were a family that took the name of Sparsholt, quickly followed by the de Caritate family, who set up the Manor of Lainston and eventually built St Peters chapel there, reputedly because they found worshipping jointly with their neighbours at St Stephens in Sparsholt too much to bear.

The Domesday Book mentions Buddlesgate, which was then the Manor incorporating Sparsholt, and refers to the adjacent Parish of Crawley as follows: 'The Bishop (of Winchester) holds Crawley in lordship himself'. This included, amongst other items, 6 villagers, 25 smallholders and 20 slaves.

In this context I was surprised to find that although slavery was abolished in all British territories in 1834, at the time of Abolition this was understood to refer to the use of African Slaves in the colonies. There does not appear to have been a similar 'Abolition' of slavery existing in England up to the late Middle Ages, when both men and women could own personal service to another, were 'un-free', i.e. unable to move home or work, or buy or sell, or change allegiance, or get married, without the permission of their owner. Originally acquired as prisoners in the never-ending wars and raids in those days, they could then be sold or bought on the open market, a practice introduced into medieval England by the Romans, followed by the Normans, and adopted by the indigenous landowners as a good way of getting cheap labour to till the soil.

My curiosity to find out when this form of slavery was abolished involved a visit to the local library, which was not able to offer a comprehensive range of works on the subject, but came up with 'The Work of Work', an anthology of works on medieval slavery by learned sources on the subject. One of these deals with 'The End of Early Medieval Slavery'[2], and starts with the quotation 'Slaves were an integral and numerically important part of English Society in the Anglo-Saxon period, yet they do not seem to have excited much attention from scholars.' The reasons for this were undoubtedly the paucity of material on the subject. The cause, however, according to the author, may have been an attempt by the Church to obliterate its early acquiescence in the practice, which is evident from the material contained in the Domesday Book.

One wonders how the Bishops were able to reconcile the use of slaves with the teachings of Christ; perhaps with some soul-searching scruples, but by and large no doubt they had to get along with their powerful parishioners, whose tithes helped to support them. In some cases, even the Bishops were known to make use of slaves on their manorial estates.

According to my above-mentioned source, slavery petered out in England between AD 900 and 1100, so it would appear that the slave ownerships listed in the Domesday Book (dated 1086) for the Manor of Buddlesgate, of which Sparsholt formed a part, were already on the decline. The mechanisms of the discontinuance of the practice are not clear, though there certainly does not appear to have been any royal or ecclesiastical edict putting an end to it. More likely the slave owners found it more productive to get their cheap labour from freed slaves who had to provide their own food and shelter.

Slavery, however, is not quite dead, perhaps not even in Sparsholt, although it exists legally only as what in common parlance is known as 'wage slavery', and not necessarily associated with tilling the soil. Another form of slavery has, however, re-emerged in England, partly fostered by the employment of illegal immigrants and the sex trade.

After William the Conqueror defeated Harold in 1066, he re-distributed the land to his supporters, and those who objected had no recourse to any law other than that of the sword. Nowadays we do have recourse to the law, but all this means is that the sword has been replaced by money, and since few of us are able to risk the costs involved in land disputes, the balance is still on the side of the establishment.

Since the Norman Conquest landownership has proliferated enormously. Under Henry VIII, the monastic estates were confiscated by the Crown and sold off to his followers, resulting in a strengthening of the Crown at the expense of the Church. In subsequent centuries land, together with power in general, was spread about a bit with the growth of democracy. The Church has (not necessarily for altruistic reasons) contributed much to this spread of ownership, unlike the Crown and the aristocracy, who have clung on to their land tenaciously. As an example of this, the Plantagenets and their descendants still own a good slice of land in Britain today, some 278,000 ha (687,000 acres) in fact.[3] There is even a connection with them in Sparsholt, albeit of fairly recent origin.

The growth of landownership in the Middle Ages was due to the further sub-division of the land given as a gift by the Crown or the Church for services rendered, or by inheritance. Eventually, due to the industrialisation of Britain, the wealth acquired by industrial (and industrious) entrepreneurs enabled these to become landowners themselves. In their climb to power they paid homage to the establishment, and becoming a landowner was accepted as being the means of attaining the first rung of the ladder leading to that exalted state. Patronage was rife, and whom you knew was more important than what you knew. This, at least, has not changed much over the centuries.

1.2 Regulatory and advisory bodies

Before launching into an investigation of who does what with the land, it is as well to have a look at the various governmental bodies which affect the activities of landowners by implementing policies adopted by parliament. In some cases this means regulations which can result in prosecutions if infringed, in other cases the landowner is encouraged to adopt these policies by means of subsidies. Further restrictions are imposed by local planning bodies with the purpose of enforcing the Town and Country Planning Acts of 1990.

The bodies involved with implementing Government policies relating to land usage are the Department for the Environment, Food and Rural Affairs (DEFRA), which also incorporates The Environment Agency and Natural England, and The Planning Authority.

In addition to these regulatory bodies there are a number

of other institutions which act in an advisory capacity to the Government and landowners, such as the Game and Wildlife Conservation Trust and the Royal Society for the Protection of Birds (RSPB).

DEFRA

After the demise, figuratively speaking, of the Ministry of Agriculture and Fisheries (or the Min of Ag and Fish, as it was affectionately known), DEFRA took over its functions. Its influence on the activities of all landowners is significant, and any account of these would be meaningless without examining DEFRA's brief and function.

An obvious point of contact for information about this body would appear to be their Public Relations Department. Unfortunately, they do not have one. But they do have a multitude of web sites from which one might dig out information, given time, or, more accurately, an immense amount of time. It would have been nice to speak to a knowledgeable representative, and put my few but pertinent questions to him or her.

Since this did not appear to be an option, I decided to write to the Secretary of State for the Environment instead. He seemed to be a good starting point, i.e. the top, but alas Mr Miliband, who held this venerable position at the time of my enquiry, was too busy fighting off admirers intent on making him Prime Minister. In his place, my enquiry was met with an unhelpful reply from the Minister for Biodiversity, whose exact relationship to Mr Miliband was not revealed in the communication (perhaps it was covered by the Data Protection Act). He stated, briefly, that his department was not funded to answer questions from the public. Thankfully no mention of any Tom, Dick or Harry here.

Further persistence with the aid of my MP did, however, result in some concessions to the Freedom of Information Act, with the result that I am now able to divulge the following to what I hope will be my grateful public:

DEFRA is an umbrella organisation incorporating numerous offspring, amongst others:

a) the Environment Agency, which is split between Bristol and London, where they set national policy, and 22 national services and 8 regional offices employing 12000 staff in total, with a total budget of about £1bn.

b) Natural England, which was formed by bringing together English Nature, the Landscape, Access and Recreation elements of the Countryside Agency, and the Environmental Land Management Functions of the Rural Development Service. It will 'work for people, places and nature, to enhance biodiversity, landscapes and wildlife in rural, urban, coastal and marine areas: promoting access, recreation and public well-being and contributing to the way natural resources are managed so that they can be enjoyed now and in the future.' This varied and extensive brief would be difficult to enunciate without stopping for breath, and is provided on the relatively modest budget of £210 million per annum. Cheap at twice the price, I should have thought, but who am I to judge?

So there we have it. Or do we? The structural set-up of DEFRA is somewhat mind-boggling, and I have made what can only be described as a foolhardy attempt to clarify it both to myself and my readers, as follows:

DEFRA Mission Statement

DEFRA's avowed mission is to get industry, government and the consumer to work together to secure a sustainable future for our farming and food industries, as viable industries contributing to a better environment and healthy and prosperous communities. Further to this, I am informed that the then (but no longer) Secretary of State responsible, set out our goal to develop a farming sector which is profitable, makes a net positive environmental contribution, and effectively manages the landscape and the natural assets that lie underneath it, including soil, water and biodiversity.

All doubtlessly laudable aims, and who should quarrel with them? Well, the taxpayer might, though it is probable that, like me, he will have no more than a mere glimmer of an idea how well, or otherwise, all our billions are used to achieve them. As for the landowners and farmers, although they are on the receiving end, I got a distinct feeling that they were not happy bunnies. The main gripe was the never-ending paperwork descending on them explaining what they should be doing to earn their subsidies, and how to claim them. So much, in fact, that some of them employ people just to deal with the paperwork.

Cynics might say the function of the state is to supply forms for us to fill in. Public servants might say they are only trying to implement what our representatives in parliament have decided is in our best interests. Many of us are acquainted with the paperwork associated with income tax, and a good many of us also employ specialists to deal with it. So why not the landowners, particularly if they are already assured of a subsidy as a result?

DEFRA costs

Chapter 9 of the DEFRA Departmental Report contains information on administrative and resource costs in terms of functions and activities performed by the Department attributable to farming. It is all on the Internet – all 256 pages of it. And here are some snippets for those who like a few figures:

Planned Public Spending for 2007/8 (rounded up to nearest £0.1 billion[4]:

	£bn
Total Spending Budget (Resource plus Capital)	3.6

Which included the following:

Environmental Protection:	2.1
Natural resources and Rural Affairs	0.6
Animal Health and Welfare	0.3
Rural Payment Agency	0.3

For those unsure of the term £billion, I hasten to confirm that I have used the current international usage which defines it as merely one thousand million pounds, and not a previous definition which had it at a million million pounds. Some readers may think that since we can't comprehend these magnitudes anyway, what does it matter? For their sake, I propose to use some more familiar items as yardsticks (or should that be metresticks) for comparison, as follows:

Total UK Planned Public Sector Current
Expenditure for 2007/8:   £538 billion[5]

Total NHS expenditure for 2006:   £76 billion[6]

Seen against these, the DEFRA spending plans look quite modest, if we accept that they represent an investment in the future in terms of safeguarding biodiversity and sustainability as well as combating global warming by promoting the production and use of bio-mass fuel.

Why DEFRA ?

One of the pleasures of moving about in unfamiliar territory is the opportunity it presents for asking all sorts of silly questions. When it comes to DEFRA, the overriding silly question would have to be 'Why DEFRA? Why can't we just leave the land to be managed by owners who respond to market forces, get rid of thousands of civil servants and cut our income taxes accordingly?

This appears to be a good question, even if I say so myself, and one I will try to address. It could be put another way: do we, the general public, really want to, or indeed need to, try to control what the landowners do with their land? And what would happen if we didn't?

An easy answer would be to say that if we didn't try to control our environment, it would quickly become a nice place for a few landowners living on large tracts of countryside with minimal access for the rest of us. Market forces dictating short term profits would entail the uncontrolled use of fertilisers and pesticides, and the grubbing out of hedgerows resulting in a diminution of wildlife, to name but a few of the possible harmful activities. Biodiversity would be out of the window, and all in all, things would take a nasty turn as far as 'we' are concerned. In short, the overriding principle would be that jam today is better than at some time in the indefinable future.

The other side of the coin is not that much better. The army of civil servants descending on the land armed with sheaves of forms may be more than just a form-filling nuisance. They may be implementing policies which are actually harmful to our future. An example of misguided government policy which springs to mind is the massive planting of conifers in the 1950s which was encouraged by government through tax incentives. Whilst there may have been good reasons for doing so at the time, the devastating effect on wildlife and biodiversity has resulted in a complete about face. In fact, the government is currently engaged in uprooting millions of trees planted in the Scottish bogs at a time when this appeared to be a good idea, but is no longer thought to be so now.

Another example of the road to hell being paved with good intentions was the rationalisation of farming for cereals for the European grain mountain, with ever increasing field sizes necessitating the grubbing out of hedgerows. Again, there has been an about turn on that policy, but only after the loss of some 58,800 miles of hedgerows between 1984 and 1990.[7] Averaged out, this amounts to 9,800 miles per annum, equivalent to about 11 times the distance from Land's End to John O'Groats.

In retrospect, then, it could be argued that in these examples the regulators have done as much harm as the landowners might have done if left free to do as they like. The Government's view would be that it did what the experts at the time advised it as being the right thing to do. In the event, and seen in hindsight, the experts weren't right. But we all have to consult specialists of one kind or another, and we are all faced with the possibility that we listened to the wrong ones, or that due to a change in circumstances, the right thing at the time turned out to be the wrong thing later on. Whatever the problem, if we ignore those who are paid to know the answer, we do so at our peril. In the last analysis, in a democracy we are at least able to argue against the accepted wisdom – and many do.

The Planning Authority

As far as landowners are concerned, this exists to implement the 1990 Town and Country Planning Act, which was designed to retain 'Green Belts' around our major conurbations. Again we have an army of public servants scrutinising not just what landowners are up to, but developers in general and even us in our homes. If you want to cut down a tree or put in double glazing, or even solar panels or a wind turbine, you need to get permission first.

This might appear to be a restriction on our freedom, but it is also undoubtedly a safeguard for those who have neither the ability nor the means to protect themselves from others who might have no compunction about having their own way and the devil take the hindmost. In addition, residential and industrial developments on greenfield sites would proliferate whenever the owners were strapped for spending money.

The Government's latest thinking about the Green Belt shows some softening in its attitude to it. The enormous pressure to provide more housing is due to the demands of an increasing population, and exacerbated by the splitting up of marriages resulting in each partner wanting their own separate home, together with the growth of single parent families. Although so-called brown sites are claimed to provide sufficient land to cope with this, these are not necessarily where people want to live. There are thus already numerous planning applications for developments in Green Belt areas to the tune of between 500 and several thousand dwellings at a time, and although landowners don't necessarily want these in their backyard, some would undoubtedly stand to gain nice little nest eggs if they come about.

Although Sparsholt landowners (apart from those known to be developers) have not been actively promoting new developments in the village, some objected to having been excluded from the envelope of the built-up area of the village as established by the local Planning Office, presumable because it would be more difficult to get planning permission for further development on land outside this envelope. This is just one immediate example of how the Planning Authority can have an important influence in a small community like Sparsholt, and it is not surprising that planning matters are one of the issues which result in good attendances at Parish Council meetings when they are on the agenda.

The Game and Wildlife Conservation Trust

This is a Charity mainly carrying out research, although it has an associated Limited Company which takes the results of its researches out on to farms and charges for the advice proffered. For those readers who, like myself, may not be wholly conversant with the term, 'Game' is defined in the Oxford English Dictionary as a collective noun for 'wild animals or birds hunted for sport or food'. The Game Conservancy informs me that this definition, also known by the name of 'Quarry', no longer encompasses all the activities of the Trust which now has a much wider brief including research into invertebrates, fish, woodland, predation, pesticides etc. In general, the objects of the Trust consist of promoting for the public benefit the conservation of game and wildlife together with the associated flora and fauna, conducting research into game and wildlife management, and educating the public and those managing the countryside in the conservation or promotion of biological diversity.

The staff of the Game Conservation Trust publish scientific papers on these subjects and give on-farm game, wildlife management and conservation advice to farmers under the auspices of the Farming and Wildlife Advisory Group FWAG, who will pay GCT for their services.

Its impact on Sparsholt may not be obvious, but on closer inspection some arable land has acquired extended field margins and areas of 'Set-aside' sometimes planted with wildlife feed. Expert advice on the management and conservation of these would fall within the remit of the Trust.

The RSPB

The RSPB is a charity originally set up under a charter granted by Edward VII in 1904. It works for the conservation of wild birds, and provides land management advice relating to this to the Government and the farming community. Although not present as such in our parish, it is no mean landowner in its own right, and, with some 131,000 ha (324,000 acres) spread over 200 nature reserves, lags closely behind the Crown Estate in the landownership league. Its 1600 staff are engaged in administering charitable activities running to an annual expenditure of £82 million. These activities entail the setting up of new nature reserves, promoting nature conservation through research, monitoring, managing nature reserves, plus advocacy and campaigning, education and public engagements. Its contacts with the farming community are maintained through getting farmers to attend advisory courses, and it promotes agricultural and environmental schemes, and aims to influence rural policy. It is also consulted on the future of the UK's woodlands and uplands, in addition to advising government on the effects of housing developments and wind farms on the wildlife environment. Its contacts with Sparsholt are limited to the occasional membership drive at the Village Hall, although bodies like the Forestry Commission and the Farley Mount Country park would be advised by it via meetings at national and County Council levels respectively.

And others

In addition to the above there are a number of other organisations which have an interest in what landowners do with their land, such as UK Biodiversity, Scottish Natural

Heritage, the Countryside Alliance, the Countryside Landowners Association, the anti-hunting lobby, animal rights campaigners, the Mammal Society, the Deer Society, the Ramblers Association and the Open Spaces Society, to name but a few. At this stage suffice to say that landowners are not short of advice, admonition or instruction on what and what not to do with their land.

1.3   Finding out who owns the land

Looking out from my upstairs windows, I can see a sizeable piece of Sparsholt. But apart from hearsay, I had little knowledge of to whom it actually belonged. The obvious point of reference appeared to be the Land Registry, which I had heard mentioned at various times as being the ultimate source of information on this matter.

The Land Registry

This came into being in 1925 with the avowed purpose 'to register ownership of land in England and Wales and to record dealings with land once it is registered', and also to 'provide easy access to up-to-date and guaranteed information about registered land'. Further investigation revealed that there are 26 Land Registry offices distributed around the country.

Fully intent on an exposé of how much their activities are costing the taxpayer, I immediately had the wind taken out of my sails when I learned that the Land Registry is 'an Executive Agency and a Trading Fund which makes no call on moneys voted by Parliament. By statute, it is required to ensure that its income from fees covers all its expenditure.' Its mission is 'to provide the world's best service for guaranteeing ownership of land and facilitating property transactions.' And who could quarrel with that?

Well, perhaps the users. But more of that later. Just a couple more figures for the nosy parkers: the chief executive takes home around £153,000k (2006), and the other 6 executive directors around £109,000, with accrued pensions of around £136,000 (each). In the private sector, that may be peanuts. So how about the other 8500 odd (no aspersions intended) employees? They have to make do with £244 million – but that's between them, of course, averaging out at just less than £29,000 each.

Now for the user bit. Finding out who owns Sparsholt turned out to be more difficult than I had expected. My first telephone enquiry to the Land Registry at Weymouth brought forth a sharp intake of breath from the other end, followed by the statement that what I was asking for was quite out of the ordinary. Had I come armed with the address and post code of the owners of the land I was interested in they could have provided full details including plans, subject of course to whether the property was actually registered or not (this does not apply to the Scottish Land Registry, which will produce a registered title from the name of the owner alone). But to start with a parish boundary and then expect the Land Registry to find out who owns parcels of land in excess of 20ha within this boundary was practically unknown.

Further probing resulted in a referral to Ordnance Survey, who, I was informed, would be able to provide the 1:1600 scale maps required by the Land Registry to even look at the enquiry seriously. Ordnance Survey however had by then privatised this service, and referred me to a local copying establishment who would be able to help.

"Ah yes," said a young man there, "we recently did one like that. Size A1, I think that was. Came to about £200". Sharp intake of breath on my part. After further consideration, this was followed by deep depression. For the size of the area in question, covering up to 25 square miles, I would in fact have needed the equivalent of 20 sheets of A1, i.e. £4000 worth.

By now I had visions of going bankrupt on this mission. Begging in the streets of Winchester, furthermore, is a highly competitive undertaking, made more daunting in my case by a vision of having old drachma coins thrown into my hat accompanied by a sneer from those less than enthusiastic about my undertaking.

On being informed of this scenario, the Registry took pity and suggested breaking up the total area of Sparsholt into 4 pieces, and dealing with these one at a time. They also offered to identify each of these pieces from a marked-up Ordnance Survey map to a scale of merely 1:16000, and to supply ten title numbers within each of these areas for free.

The title number is the number allocated by the Registry at the time of registration. It is the key to the required documents, which will consist of a copy of the register entries with the full address of the property, the names of the registered owner(s) together with details of any restrictions or covenants pertaining to the use of the land. In addition, and only if specifically ordered, the Registry will supply a detailed plan of the property outlined in colour, to enable it to be identified on the ground. The current cost of this is £4.00 for the Register copy and £4.00 for the plan, if ordered by post. Both of these items can now be downloaded from the Registry Internet web page (www.landregistry.co.uk) at the price of £3.00 each.

On the face of it, these appear modest investments for gaining all this invaluable information, but it has to be seen in the context of the Registry's total fee income in 2007 being £464 million, with an operating surplus of £90 million. One can only conjecture that the average punter's curiosity far exceeds my own, otherwise it would mean that more than half the population spends ten pounds per annum to find out who owns what, not a very likely scenario.

But why worry about that, things were definitely brightening up for me. Bankruptcy had receded into the middle distance, we were now talking just in terms of tens of pounds rather than hundreds, not sufficient of course to keep the Land Registry in the style to which they might have become accustomed, but I found myself unable to lose any sleep over that.

There is one important point to remember when undertaking a search of this kind with the Land Registry: if the land in question incorporates smaller properties which would not be of interest, then in order to limit the number of titles to be investigated, it will be necessary to outline the principal larger areas incorporating as few properties as possible.

The reason for this is that there is always the danger that each one of these may have its own land title and not belong to the owner of the land to be searched. Alternatively, the areas containing significant numbers of dwellings could be outlined with the request to exclude them from the search.

If the postal address and postal code of the property are known, the Land Registry will be able to supply the relevant title number together with the documents referred to if the property is registered. In this context it may be noted that nosy parkers will be able to establish what their neighbour's property fetched when sold, and not too long after the event, either.

The whole idea of compulsory registration originated in the London area in the 1920s, and has only gradually spread to most parts of the country, reaching, for example, the area of the Weymouth Registry (my 'local' Registry Office) as late as the 1990s. I took time off to visit there, and met one of the knowledgeable people I had been bothering on the phone and via post and fax over a number of months. After an hour's conversation I felt more confident in pursuing my quest, and was supplied with a comprehensive set of leaflets about the Land Registry containing information on how to use their service, together with information on the location of their 26 offices.

Having got this far, the rest appeared to be easy sailing. Just get hold of the registered titles in the area, and the relevant entries in the Land Register will do the rest. This seemed too good to be true. It was too good to be true. The very first title received referred to the registered owner as being 'The Minister of Agriculture Fisheries and Food'. Quite apart from the minister being referred to as the owner, it begged the question as to what has happened to him, because no such minister now exists. The Land Registry disclaimed all responsibility on the basis that their information was correct at the date of registration, and if the new proprietor has not re-registered the property, there is nothing they can do about it. This shows that the hard-won information from the Land

Registry is not necessarily up to date, even though it may have been so at the time of registration.

A further hurdle materialised when, after locating around fifteen titles to major land holdings, there remained some 50% of the parish land not accounted for. The explanation from the Land Registry was simple: this land has not been registered. Why? Well, if there has not been any change in ownership since about 1988, no registration would have resulted, since compulsory registration of new land transactions in this area only came into being at that time. As recently as 2000, there were an estimated two million unregistered estates in England and Wales.

All this seems almost medieval, and a surprising lapse from the previous attempt to produce a complete register of landowners in 1874-6, entitled *The Return of Owners of Land in England, Scotland, Ireland and Wales,* which resulted in the registration of 95% of the land of Great Britain. So what has happened to change all that in the interim? The overriding answer can only be that landowners did not consider it to be in their best interests to continue filing returns, and gradually due to the breaking up of larger estates by inheritance or sale almost half the land registered in 1872 is not listed on the current register.

And Other Sources

After nine months intermittent research, I had established the ownership, subject to the preceding caution, of about 50% of the land area of Sparsholt. Not, you might rightly comment, a good return on my time, but I was at least not on the road to bankruptcy (yet!). I had however struck the real stumbling block which the Registry had repeatedly expressed caution on: not all the land is registered. This applies to both private and public landowners. So where does one go from here?

This is where I hit on an idea which seemed more promising. Having waxed lyrical about the 'Return of Owners of Land', why not get hold of a copy of it? After all, at least some of the land holdings in the parish might not have changed ownership since 1876. Some of them would, of course, but it might still make a dent in the remaining 50% of the parish land not accounted for.

This resulted in an expedition to the local Reference Library, who very promptly produced a copy of the 'Return' consisting of a number of bulky volumes. My first mistake was to draw attention to the Library Staff that the Hampshire section was missing from the tomes, only to be informed that at the time of the making of 'The Return' Hampshire was incorporated with 'Southampton'.

'Whoops' said I, covered in embarrassment. This quickly turned to chagrin as I delved into the section dealing with Southampton, which contained a list of names of landowners in alphabetical order, together with their place of residence and the amount of land they owned, with never a clue as to the location of it beyond that it lay in the county of 'Southampton.' A further mere detail missing was the full address of the owner. So, for example, the address of one 'Abbercrombie, David', credited with owning 143 acres, was given as 'London', and this simple method of identification applied to most names in the book, with certain exceptions, presumably for owners of stature, such as for example 'Bathurst, Sir Frederick' whose address is given as 'Clarendon Park, Wiltshire'.

Higher up on this scale I would have expected to find 'Victoria, Queen, of Buckingham Palace, London'. This, it turned out, would have been somewhat too familiar. What I found listed instead was 'Crown Property, Whitehall, 6550 acres'. So the crown owned, or even owns, all this land in Southampton, now known as Hampshire. Interesting, but exactly whereabouts in Hampshire? And similarly tantalising, 'Dean and Chapter of Winchester, 6550 acres'. The only possibility of following up these clues would be to contact the current tenants of these titles.

In the case of the Queen I had little reason to think she still owns any part of Sparsholt, but abandoned any attempt to verify this assumption by writing to her in case I got on to the Duke's hit list. The Dean and Chapter however was another matter altogether, since he (or they?) had already surfaced several times during my researches, and I accordingly approached him (or them) with the results accounted for under the heading of 'The Church' in Part 5.2.

Just tracking down the private landowners proved to be a problem. One could enquire from adjacent known landowners, for example. But I didn't know any of the local landowners, at least not well enough to ask them to tell me just which land was theirs. So that left public records of one kind or another. But what kind? Or I might have disported myself in the middle of a field or walked into woodland armed with a shotgun and waited to be challenged by the real owner or his representative. Since this was not my style, and I don't in any case own a shotgun, I was at a loss how to proceed. And then I hit on the answer: the grapevine! This entails asking everybody that you know if they know who owns this field or that wood. It's quite surprising how soon the relevant information materialises.

Since I lacked the temerity of asking to see their deeds, however, it could be said that about half of the landownership attributed in the following chapters is not corroborated, and will remain so until the land is registered. Another problem was that since some of the land in the parish is leased to locals by absentee landowners, the lessor will have to be tracked down, which, as mentioned previously, founders on the Data Protection Act.

Even having tracked down your landowner, how do you get him to own up? This is, of course, a matter of personal diplomacy, a social connection being the most likely method. Failing this, a direct contact by phone worked in some cases, on the basis that "I am doing research on landownership in the parish, and would they kindly give me a few minutes of their time to discuss matters pertaining to this in as far as it affects fellow parishioners". The success rate of this approach was good, but has left some gaps resulting from landowners who took the 'mind your own business' attitude.

Part 2

The Private Landowners

50% of the land area of the civil parish of Sparsholt is owned by just eight private landowners. Before commencing on my quest to find out about their background and what they did on their land, I already knew that the stereotype ex-public school hunting and shooting type landed gentry with a land-owning pedigree as long as your arm was not known in the parish. Pity really, since it would have been far more exciting to generate a little adrenalin with the commoners lined up against the aristocracy, with a little blood sport debate bolstered up by anti-hunting sentiments to add spice, and with a jaundiced look at (in Oscar Wilde's words) 'the unspeakable in pursuit of the uneatable'. But apart from a bit of pheasant and partridge shooting, I was unable to establish any controversial activities, not even drag hunting, although this still goes on in the neighbouring parish of Hursley.

Sparsholt does however have a connection with the land-owning aristocracy, albeit a tenuous one, in Lady Julia Craig Harvey, the wife Nicholas Craig Harvey, of Lainston Farm. By virtue of being a daughter of the previous Duke of Northumberland, she can claim to be a Plantagenet descendant. Apart from that, none of the landowners in Sparsholt that I have spoken to can claim to be related to a power in the land, nor to the best of my knowledge can any of those I only have second-hand information on. Although most of them inherited their land, only one has a farming history in his family going back more than two generations.

2.1 The Major Landowners

This classification is simply based on the relative size of landholdings of the owner in the Parish, though some of the owners mentioned may (and some definitely do) own land in one of the adjoining parishes or even elsewhere. Of the five major landholders listed, the largest one owns nearly 20% and the smallest just over 2% of the parish land.

Moor Court Farm

The largest landowner in the Parish is Philip Meitner, of Moor Court Farm, with some 19.6% of the total parish land area, some of it jointly owned. A relative newcomer to Sparsholt, he has been in farming all his life, and came to Sparsholt in1975. He acquired Moor Court from the Church, who had owned it since the dissolution of the monasteries by Henry VIII. His family originally came from Czechoslovakia where his great grandfather was a landowner. Among a family of distinguished scientists his aunt, Lise Meitner, was an atomic physicist and received the Nobel Prize for atomic research posthumously in 1999.

Philip Meitner farms together with his son-in-law Andrew Osmond, who lives at Moor Court Farmhouse. Meitner's daughter Sarah Osmond leases another 6.2 % of the Parish Land from the Martineau Will Trust, bringing the total land farmed by the family up to nearly 26% of the total parish land.

In earlier years Philip Meitner kept a dairy herd of 300 cows and 200 young stock, but now the farms are largely arable. In the winter months turnips are grown as keep for several thousand store lambs.

Lainston Farm
Next in line in size of landholding in the parish is Nicholas Craig Harvey, of Lainston Farm, with 13.7% of the parish land. In addition, he owns and farms land in the adjoining parish of Crawley. He has lived in the parish all his life, originally in Lainston House (now Lainston House Hotel – see below), which was acquired by his grandfather, an industrialist engaged in the manufacture of cotton spinning mills, in 1920. He now lives in Lainston Dairy, named after what it actually was until circa 1965.

Although involved in the running of Lainston Farm, his other occupations include being a director of Lainston Estates and a merchant bank, in addition to being chair of the charity 'Victim Support' in Hampshire and a governor of Sparsholt Primary School. He jointly manages Lainston Farm with Richard Monk (see below) who farms some of the adjacent land.

Craig Harvey has also been a parish councillor for some years, and is married to a daughter of the Duke of Northumberland. Her brother, the present Duke, owns some 45,000 ha (111,000 acres) and can be classed as one of the principal private landowners in the country. It could be argued, therefore, that the Plantagenets now have a toehold (or should that be 'Spousehold') in Sparsholt!

The land belonging to Craig Harvey in Sparsholt is principally used for arable crops.

He raises pheasants and partridges for shooting purely as a social function, and until recently received subsidies on some 8% of his land classified as 'set aside'.

Rookley Farm

Next in line is the Monk family, of Rookley Farm, Up Somborne, with some 110 ha within Sparsholt plus a further 374 ha in the adjoining parish of Crawley, where they also rent or contract-farm an additional 420 ha. Richard Monk, the current manager, is a third generation farmer. His mother came from a farming family at Andover where she met his father Tony before taking on Rookley Farm. Richard Monk also farms Craig Harvey's land in Sparsholt on a joint venture basis, which would bring the total of his farming activities to extend to some 20% of the Parish land area. Next to Philip Meitner he could therefore be said to be one of the most significant farming figures in Sparsholt, although he resides just outside the Parish Boundary.

Richard Monk spent some time working as a land agent before joining his father in the family business, A.F. Monk (Rookley) Ltd, which specialises in the production of seed for all types of arable crops with a small portion devoted to poppies grown as a commercial crop for the manufacture of morphine based products. This also applies to the land the family acquired in Sparsholt in 1979. The company has its own seed testing laboratory licensed by DEFRA. They have nine employees, three times the average for the area. The family have farmed the area since 1960, but had farmed in the Andover area before that.

The land farmed by Richard Monk for Craig Harvey in Sparsholt produces commercial arable corps, the growing of seed for wheat, barley, oats and grass taking place outside the parish. The processing of seed is a specialised operation involving a cleaning and sorting plant and a test laboratory. In addition, the farm is responsible for some 26 ha of set-aside land (see under DEFRA), and is licensed to grow opium for use as diamorphine by the NHS (illustrations 1a and 1b)

Richard Monk's land in Sparsholt does not have any organised shooting taking place over it. The other land he farms has shoots organised by the other landowners or tenants. Much of his land is covered by various DEFRA environmental schemes such as Entry Level Scheme, Countryside Stewardship Scheme and Farm Woodland Scheme. The land he farms for Lainston Estate is also covered by some of these schemes. In addition Richard Monk promotes wildlife in other ways such as providing owl nesting boxes in the barns on his land and providing wide verges and strips to encourage a diverse wildlife habitat.

The David Martineau Will Trust
Finding out about this took a disproportionate amount of time because it is neither registered nor traceable by the normal procedures. Although it was common knowledge in the parish that the Martineau Trust owns a sizeable portion of it, it was only after tracking down their land agent by hearsay that I was able to ascertain just what this amounted to (just over 6% in fact), and that the bulk of it was leased to Sarah Osmond, the daughter of Philip Meitner, as already mentioned above.

The local Agent of the Martineau Trust also informed me that the Trust Deed setting out the Trustees' responsibilities is a private document, and that the Estate is held in trust for the five descendants of the Martineau family, three of whom reside in America. The Trust's principal aims for its landed property were 'sound estate management' and the development of their land in Sparsholt in the medium or long term future.

This, I thought, was an exceedingly frank admission which might make the residents of adjoining properties a little nervous about what the future may hold, and if not giving them sleepless nights would at least stimulate them to scan local planning applications carefully. In the interim between 'now' and 'the medium term' the Trust has leased land to the primary school for a sports ground, sold land for the construction of Bostock Close (a Housing Association Development in the village) and created a permissive way from this to the school. My attempts to interview the members of the Trust with a view to establishing where and how they see future developments have remained unsuccessful.

This brings me back to the Introduction, where I mentioned the statement that, as a mere Tom, Dick or even Harry, I had no need for this sort of information. Since a part of the self-imposed mission of this book is to inform readers about the origin and influence of our landowners, I felt obliged to pursue my objective on the basis that any information from individuals whose activities have a profound effect on a lot of people and their environment should be in the public domain.

and Others

Other major private landowners in the parish not accounted for either did not reply to requests for an interview, or declined it. However, looking at their land from the nearest public right of way, and bolstered by hearsay, it would appear they use their land mostly for grazing horses and cattle, and also providing stabling and paddocks for local horse owners, in one instance also for breeding and bringing on horses for racing.

2.2   The Minor Landowners

Under these I have listed private landholdings below 30ha In size. It will be noted that I have more to say about these than the larger landowners, and I can only ascribe this to the following factors:

a) Their activities have a day to day association with the parish.

b) They employ more permanent staff, some from the parish.

c) They were prepared to discuss their activities at length.

Lainston House Hotel

Set amongst extensive fields, woodland and tree avenues, Lainston House Hotel is undoubtedly one of the Country's top country house hotels. I can vouch for this, since in addition to being an occasional dinner guest I have actually stayed there to celebrate a second honeymoon. For all I know, Mrs Thatcher and ex President George Bush senior (not 'W') may have slept in the same bed as us, though not (so I have been reliably in formed) at the same time or for the same reason. George Bush, I should add, is not related to me, and he might of course regret this if he knew, particularly in view of our shared experience of Lainston House Hotel.

This now belongs to the 'Exclusive Hotels' group, and is

owned by the Pecorelli family, who have several hotels spread about the South of England. Its grounds occupy about 25 ha (63 acres), most of which consists of grassland bordered by mature trees, including the 18th century Lime Avenue which stretches from the rear of the hotel for about 1km, and incorporates a helicopter pad just below its terrace. Its extensive grassland is kept well manicured by a staff of gardeners, with the help of an occasional harvesting operation by the adjacent Sparsholt College to supplement the silage supplies for the college farm. The college also provides the hotel with other services such as tree surgery as part of its student training. Since some of the gardening staff received their training at the college, this seems to be an admirable arrangement.

Apart from providing a grass crop, the larger grassland areas are used for entertainments ranging from clay-pigeon shooting through archery and falconry to goose herding. Or was it goosing? Who knows what the idle rich do for entertainment these days. Well, of course, there's always fly-fishing on the nearby River Test where fishermen can have a whale of a time (or should that be 'trout of a time') accompanied, according to the hotel web page, by their personal Ghillie (variant spelling of 'Gillie', meaning an attendant or guide for hunting) and with additional base support from the hotel through regular visits of menials to provide bacon sandwiches or even a fully fledged riverside barbeque to revive those who may be suffering from trout-tickling fatigue.

For those guests who are into less active pursuits, or who have had their fill of trout tickling and goose herding (or goosing) and need something to fill the interminable gap between Tea and Happy Hour, there is a wealth of historical

1a   Opium in Sparsholt : poppies in flower

1b   and Richard Monk watching the opium combine at work

2 Lainston House Hotel: Manager Cliff Hasler (helicopter pad hidden in middle distance)

features to take in, ranging from the adjacent remains of St Peter's chapel where the bigamous marriage of the notorious Elizabeth Chudley, Duchess of Kingston, took place, to the pet cemetery where the previous owners, the Craig Harveys, lovingly interred their dogs under inscribed and dated nameplates. Then there is the historic dovecote lined with chalk bricks excavated during the digging of the adjacent well.

My brief visit to the latter has left a lasting impression on me, occasioned by looking down into the well which is reputedly 300ft deep. In spite of efforts with cables and torches no one has actually seen the bottom. Since the viewing access hatch is big enough to permit an easy way down (and out, for anyone tired of this life), one wonders how many skeletons they will find at the bottom if they ever get down there.

For anyone viewing, it might be advisable to be on good terms with the person behind, since even a slight accidental bump from that region would be enough to propel one on an irreversible course. I would guess that one would even be out of earshot of any feigned apologetic exclamation such as 'sorry' or 'whoops' by the time it was uttered.

There is also a rotating gantry consisting of a massive oak pillar and oak beams which was powered by a donkey walking around in circles to haul up the water in buckets. This was later abandoned when they installed a steam engine to do the donkey work just to provide water for one family and its retainers. Guests can read about all this and more in a local history booklet available to them, originally compiled by Valery Barnes, a villager and in addition retainer of the Hotel of many years standing.

Amongst crops grown in the grounds are products of the recently established vegetable garden and greenhouse, providing organically grown vegetables and herbs exclusively for use by the hotel kitchen for eventual consumption by the hotel guests.

Apart from thus pleasing its guests the hotel fulfils a local social function by being one of the largest employers in the parish, with 87 full-time and 6 part-time employees. Many of these come from other countries, some from as far away as Australia. Apart from core staff, the average stay of employees is between two and three years. In addition to this the hotel contributes to the local economy by its policy of sourcing supplies from as close as possible. This policy has led to the establishment of a bakery on the premises which also sells its products through local outlets including the local shop and post office, and the Farmers market in Winchester.

All this is under the management of 40 year old Cliff Hasler (illustration 2) who has been in the hotel business for most of his life. He told me that Lainston House was acquired from the Craig Harvey family (see *Private Landowners*) for conversion into a hotel by the then manager of the London Dorchester hotel in 1986, but re-sold shortly thereafter to the Pecorelli family, who have remained its owners ever since. The family still monitor the running of the hotel by monthly visits from Mr. Pecorelli, who is the managing director.

A glance at the wider scene reveals that the total annual income of hotels in Britain in 2004/5 was £10.3 billion[1]. This may be chickenfeed seen in terms of the UKs gross domestic product, currently running at around £1300 billion, i.e. the hotels' contribution was less than 1%, but every little helps.

Kirton Farm Nurseries

My dictionary defines horticulture as the cultivation of vegetables, which is also known as market gardening, and fruit for food, as well as the growing of trees, shrubs and other plants for ornamental purposes. Under this definition, but excluding peas and potatoes as being 'arable' crops grown on larger fields, this activity currently accounts for about just under 4% of the total crop area in Britain.

Kirton Farm comes under the ornamental section of horticulture. Set up in 1984 by Derek and Caroline Taylor (the latter a member of the Monk family which owns the adjacent land), it grows herbaceous perennials and micropropagated herbaceous plants which they market through local supermarkets and garden centres. They describe their activities as 'balancing ethical, environmental and commercial interests', and this applies particularly to their recent branching out into a niche market with their environmentally friendly 'Hairy Pot Plants', which are simply plants grown in coconut fibre pots imported from India. In adopting these containers they are doing away with the ubiquitous plastic trays as well as providing the plant roots with a decomposing container, all features designed to endear them to the green community which is willing to pay the additional cost.

Another side of the business is engaged in the production of micropropagated plants in the laboratory. The four hectare site is largely occupied by the net-sided plastic tunnels in which all the plants are grown. Their eco-friendly claims are further reinforced by use of waste, natural and organic materials, and the re-cycling of card boxes and pots after planting. The sub-irrigated sand beds on which the plants are grown have numerous benefits including greatly reduced water usage. A system of low-compost leaching means lower levels of fertilizer required, and the special sand-bed covers used deter slugs and weeds, thus reducing the need for chemical control. Movement of plants etc. around the site is carried out by means of electric buggies.

Derek and Caroline met at Chelmsford Agricultural College as students, and set up the business together. Their green and ethical credentials are further reinforced by their commitment to an organization co-founded by them under the name of SCION, which is aimed at the ethical sourcing and training of legal immigrants. They currently employ the equivalent of ten full-time staff.

And Others

The owners of the remaining minor landholdings were either not traceable, or declined to be interviewed. Their land, from cursory inspection, is uncultivated and principally used as grazing for cattle, sheep or horses.

2.3 Subsidies

Most farmers nowadays receive subsidies of one kind or another. The question of why we subsidise farming is debatable. It could be argued that we pay farmers for not ruining our environment. But surely they can be trusted to adopt socially responsible practices without the need for an army of civil servants to police them and offer them bribes in the way of subsidies for this, that and the other environmental action? My answer: human nature and the lowest common denominator would soon destroy any vestige of civilisation if we were all free to do what 'we', as opposed to 'them' deem to be right. If there is a problem with regulations, it has to be whether we consider them to be in our interests or not, and even in a democratic society there are always bound to be some who feel they are being hard done by.

A good example of unpopular legislation is the parking restrictions we are all subject to, yet what would happen if we were free to park our cars where it suited us in our towns and cities? If we weren't all faced with punitive fines for parking illegally, chaos would quickly result. Everybody would want to park in the High street next to Marks and Spencers or Sainsbury's or whatever, if necessary on the pavement. A free-for all would result in the survival of the fittest parkers, with everybody carrying weapons in their vehicles to defend their god-given rights.

Even without taking too pessimistic a view of human nature, we have to accept that regulations are an essential part of our civilisation, and that this applies as much in the countryside as it does in urban areas. One significant difference in the parking regulation comparison is that whilst many of us have had to pay a parking fine, I have never heard of a landowner being fined for breaking regulations in my area. This can only have one of two explanations: a) they have never broken regulations, or b) they haven't been caught doing so.

My question as to what subsidies are available as incentives to landowners and farmers to collaborate with DEFRA, and what the current annual subsidies were, drew the response that they were not required to deal with this kind of request if the information was already available on the internet. Which it was – well, sort of, via a hyperlink on the internet containing some 120 symbols and digits.

However, after some persistence, I was actually given a figure of total farming subsidies for the parish of Sparsholt in 2006. It came to £66,000 in total(1), which works out at approximately £80 per hectare (£32 per acre) of cultivated land. This would seem a modest amount, but of course it depends on the size of the landholdings. For those owning in excess of 200 ha (500 acres), we are talking in terms of £16,000 per annum and over, a sum not be sneezed at by many. And for really big farmers astute enough to take their subsidies in euros and selling their future entitlements in the futures market, top end payments can amount to £250,000 and up[2].

Farmers may well claim that the subsidies they get are simply payments for services rendered, even where these just consist of not cultivating some of their land (i.e. 'set aside'). For an 'aside' on the general principle of agricultural subsidies I cannot fail but mention here that in the days when I was engaged in running a manufacturing company, I often cast an envious glance at the way agriculture was cosseted by government whilst industrial companies were permanently under threat of going to the wall if they hit a bad patch.

But things have changed again since I started writing this book. The various subsidies available to farmers have been replaced by a 'Single Payment Scheme', which, we are informed 'is the principal agricultural subsidy scheme in the European Union.' Under this scheme farmers have greater freedom to farm to the demands of the market as subsidies are no longer linked to production, and environmentally friendly farming practices (known as cross-compliance) are better acknowledged. In effect the scheme simply subsidises farmers pro rata to the land area they farm, provided they comply with the qualifying conditions that the land must be kept in good order, and must conform to 'Cross-compliance'. This is aimed at simplifying the award of subsidies, which amounted to a grand total for the UK of £2.29bn in 2007, with a recent 2006/7 survey equating this to £45,000 per claimant on average.[3]

The original idea of subsidising 'our landscape' to keep ever larger areas of 'set-aside', and discourage food production in an era of plenty, has now been abandoned. With current wheat and barley prices shooting up, the subsidies will soon fail to be of interest to many farmers, nor will the threat of global warming. Food production will be the driving force on the land, and global warming will take second place, with bio-fuel and bio-mass crops on the ascendant.

2.4 Where we have our say

This heading alone may well raise hackles in some quarters. Why should anyone, and particularly a Tom, Dick or Harry, have any say in what a landowner does with his land? And how would we like it if our neighbours told us what we can or can't do in our garden? Not much, of course, would be the answer. However, if I inundated them with bonfire smoke or barbecue smells or had my speakers blasting out rock music in my garden, or grew a 30 metre cypress alongside my fence, I could hardly object if they did the same to me. In that case, some form of enforceable regulations are considered a reasonable curtailment of our freedom. so why shouldn't this principle apply to landowners as well?

So when it comes to the landowners, what would we want to have a say about? Well, we wouldn't want them to spoil the environment by ripping out hedgerows or using excessive pesticides or cutting down trees or blocking off public rights of way or putting up a processing factory or a housing development on their land. But, you might say, there are already regulations to stop them doing any of these things. Precisely, and you may rest assured they weren't made by the landowners.

Another example of public opinion having resulted in legislation affecting landowners was the prohibition of foxhunting. It could be argued that shooting might eventually be included as well. I have to admit to a sneaking sympathy with animal rights campaigners after witnessing the bereavement of Fred the pheasant who had been patronising our garden accompanied by his three spouses. Now, at the end of the shooting season, he comes on his own, and I sometimes see him sitting on our garden bench, sodden and forlorn, staring into the middle distance. Certainly the idea of breeding these birds for the sole purpose of giving some of us pleasure in using our skill at blasting them out of the sky does not attract me for one.

Since the landowners' activities are generally covered by national regulations, local Councils are not as a rule involved, except in the case of local bye-laws, so trying to have a say via your local Council would not normally be applicable. When it comes to amending existing or introducing new nationwide regulations, that would be a matter for the Government through its numerous departments, which would ultimately be monitored by parliament. If you feel strongly enough on any issue, the only effective option is to join a pressure group that is already lobbying for what you have in mind. Getting your MP involved is another option, but unless he belongs to a party which already has your proposal in its programme, this will not be a very effective option. Neither will writing to the Prime Minister, for that matter, unless this exercise helps you to lower your blood pressure by letting off some steam.

Part 3

The Public Landowners

Within the context of this book, the term 'Public Landowners' will mean public authorities who own land to enable them to carry out tasks allocated by government and/or local authorities. In terms of accountability to the local and wider community, I have selected the local managers of public land as being my source of information, although it will be appreciated that ultimately they are responsible to a higher authority, by which, in this context, I am not referring to God, but someone nearly as exalted, i.e. a senior government or local authority official.

The public authorities which own significant areas of land in Sparsholt are the Forestry Commission (a branch of DEFRA), which owns West Wood and leases an adjacent piece of woodland, and Hampshire County Council which owns Crab Wood (a part of Farley Mount Country Park) and has a lease on Pitt Down, a small part of which falls within the Sparsholt Parish Boundary. Then there is Sparsholt College, which belongs to a trust set up by Hampshire County Council.

Smaller parcels of land included in this survey by way of highlighting public land usage of specific social interest to the local community are Ham Green Common (administered by Sparsholt Parish Council) and the village playground. As with the other smaller land holdings of charities and institutions described in the following chapter, it will become apparent that their social significance has been largely influenced by a small group of people I like to refer to as 'the movers and shakers', whose efforts are seldom rewarded by public recognition, but who form an important part of the fabric of society.

Broadly speaking, within the terms defined above, public land accounts for 33% of the land area of the Parish of Sparsholt, and in this respect is not representative of the UK as a whole, where public land accounts for only 6.4%.

3.1   The Forestry Commission

West Wood, the largest piece of public land in Sparsholt, was identified by the Land Registry as belonging to 'The Minister of Agriculture, Fisheries and Food of Whitehall Place, London, SW1A 2EY', with a note stating that the transfer of the land in this title took place between St Martins Property Investments Ltd (Transferors), a London based Investment Group, and the Minister in April 1996. This was certainly good news for those of us who think that the management of our local environment should be more responsive to the people it affects.

My efforts to establish contact with the 'Minister of Ag and Fish', however, were nipped in the bud at an early stage when it became apparent that he no longer existed (not under this title, anyway). The Land Registry were unable to make any suggestions in respect of the actual current owner since they had not been informed of any further transactions with regard to this land. The idea that owners of land, once registered, are obliged by law to inform the Land Registry of any changes in ownership does not seem to have crossed anybody's mind. Or perhaps it had, but Governments, of whatever hue, are exempt.

More researches eventually revealed that all responsibilities (and presumably rights) vested in the Minister of Ag and Fish were transferred to DEFRA (the Department of the Environment, Food and Rural Affairs) in March of 2002. The last holder of this office, one Douglas Hogg, may never have realised that he was once the owner of West Wood in Sparsholt. Or perhaps he still is? Certainly my further email and subsequent phone enquiry to DEFRA about their ownership drew an uncertain response.

My enquiry was simply whether they did in fact own West Wood. My respondent replied that the Secretary of State had more important things to concern herself with. On my suggestion that somebody there must surely know, I was told that if it was a wood it was probably Forestry Commission. But might it not belong to Hampshire County Council as part of Farley Mount Country Park?

"Ask the Land Registry."

"But I told you the Land Registry have already established it belongs to the Minister of Ag and Fish."

"The Minister of Agriculture and Fisheries doesn't exist any more."

"I know, that's what I said at the beginning."

"Well give us your e-mail address and we'll come back to you."

Which they did. West Wood is now owned by the Forestry Commission. An e-mail from DEFRA conveying this information also suggested that I address any further correspondence to the Forestry Commission. Which I did.

The Forestry Commission Map showing the extent of their land (or the land belonging to DEFRA) at West Wood failed to show some black holes in the middle of it which are not registered as belonging to it. This started another investigation which is still on-going to date. Even recent research by the Hampshire County Council Recreation and Heritage Department in connection with a claim for a footpath across one of these black holes has not positively identified the original owner, though the Dean and Chapter of Winchester Cathedral were high on the list of suspects. Whoever it is, does this mean DEFRA is in fact a squatter? Nobody out there seems to know. One could pursue the matter, but conscience forbids; why should I help to make some lawyer rich at taxpayer's expense?

Historically, the Forestry Commission has only existed since 1919. Although the biggest single landholder in Great Britain with over 1 million ha (2.6million acres) in 2000, it is apparently impossible to find out how much of this it actually owns. Surprising? Well hardly, in view of the above mentioned Min of Ag and Fish debacle. If this is the situation concerning public land, it is unlikely to be any better in the private sector, particularly if the total area of unregistered land in Britain is estimated at between 30% and 50%. None of this is helped by the Forestry Commission's refusal to disclose the identity of the buyers and details of sale of some 81,000 ha (200,000 acres) it sold between 1987 and 1995[1]

The Forestry Commission was formed in order to make Britain less vulnerable to foreign timber imports in time of war, having been progressively denuded of forests from the Elizabethan era onwards. In spite of huge land acquisitions for planting commencing after its formation, the second world war led to felling of ancient woodlands such as the New Forest, which by the end of the war had provided some 12.5 million cubic feet of timber, just about a quarter of the total amount used.

Since before the 2nd world war the Forestry Commission has been involved with a policy of planting conifers, particularly Sitka spruce, which has turned out to be an environmental disaster in terms of its effects on biodiversity. This fast growing species was closely planted on every available open space and mountainside, resulting in an unprecedented loss of wildlife cover, with the justification of giving a quicker return on investment than native species.

By the fifties, the total area of these conifer forests had more than doubled to 310,000 ha from 150,000 ha in 1939. Private companies jumped on to the bandwagon assisted by government incentives in the way of planting subsidies and tax concessions (abolished in 1988). Even peat bogs in the north of Scotland were not saved from the scourge of the Sitka spruce. When the environmental lobby finally raised the alarm, it was too late. Now the RSPB, assisted by EU funding, has felled about 4 million trees to rot in the bogs and hopefully restore these to what they were[2].

Although the number of conifers in our local West Wood is modest in comparison, even here the Forestry Commission has had to take drastic action in the hope of restoring native species and wildlife. The resultant extensive felling has drawn criticisms from those members of the local community who are regular visitors to the wood, a situation which I conjecture might have been avoided if the Parish Council had been informed in advance of the reasons for this operation.

This lack of communication with the public here is reflected on the national scale, and I quote from 'Who Owns

Scotland' by Andy Wightman: "Unlike most other European Countries, which not only consider the ownership of forests to matter a great deal and collect and publish extensive data on the subject, the Forestry Commission collects minimal information on forestry holdings and publishes nothing." With a total annual expenditure in 2006-7 of £2.3 billion[3], one would have thought there was some obligation to let us know exactly where their, or more accurately our, land is.

A reference to the current Forestry Commission web site indicates that there has been a move to keep the public abreast with recent publications from Forestry Research dealing with the recreational aspects of woodland. There is, however, no mention of West Wood as a recreational site, which in view of its size and proximity to Winchester and Southampton is a significant oversight.

Since meeting the local beat manager, I have been informed that as far as the Forestry Commission's activities in West Wood are concerned, we may take it that these are covered by the following national guidelines:

Mission Statement: to protect and expand Britain's forests and woodlands and increase their value to society and the environment.
Objective: to take the lead in the development and promotion of sustainable forest management and to support its achievement nationally.

According to the Forestry Commission's web site, it is controlled by a board of Commissioners consisting of the Chairman and up to ten Commissioners including the

Director General, all with powers prescribed by statute, who are appointed by the Queen on the advice of her ministers. The organisation also has an executive board which assists the Director General and the Country Directors, one each for England, Scotland and Wales, who are also members of the GB Board of Commissioners, and who lead the respective National Committees. It also has three executive agencies: Forest Enterprise England, Forest Enterprise Scotland and Forest Research.

It is reputedly the biggest landowner in Britain, though the evidence is difficult to get at. In 2003-4 the top-earning Executive Forestry Commissioner took home around £112,000[4], which in today's private sector equivalent might be regarded as chickenfeed, even though intervening inflation might well have pushed this up to over twice this amount.

For additional 'on the ground' information I felt reasonably relaxed about approaching their local manager, Nick Hazlitt, to tell me something about Forestry Commission activities in West Wood. After all, in spite of being economical regarding information about the extent of their holdings, the Forestry Commission is not a secret society (so I kept telling myself). On the other hand, perhaps they engage in some sort of pagan rite ('deforestration'?) which might result in a headline in the Hampshire Chronicle such as *Body of aspiring author found in woodland not far from home!*

As a precaution, however, my first meeting with Mr Hazlitt was in fact arranged in my own home. He arrived without a chainsaw and armed only with a supply of maps and information booklets about the Commission.

Nick Hazlitt has had experience in woodland management

3a   West Wood : before the holocaust

3b   and after

4a   Size comparison: Golden Retriever with muntjac deer

4b   and muntjac with Iberian lynx, a possible predator

going back some 17 years. A born and bred local Hampshire man, his work experience prior to attending Sparsholt College included a spell on the Rothschilds' Exbury Estate before working as a voluntary ranger at Crabwood and Danebury sites under a Hampshire County Council work experience scheme, together with some years employed by a forestry contractor in the survey of woodland and timber before joining the Forestry Commission. It turned out that he doesn't just manage West Wood, but another 25 woodland sites in West Hampshire and Berkshire with a total of over 3240 ha (8000 acres). The West Wood site accounts for some 260 ha (640 acres), 9% of which are leased.

He is assisted by two works supervisors and seven wildlife rangers, in addition to obtaining free services from students at Sparsholt College as part of their training. His domain, West Hampshire, with its office at Micheldever, forms a part of the South East England district, which has 78 employees.

He sees his brief as the regeneration of woodland, with the aim of thinning the conifer content to make up no more than 10% of the total, with the balance consisting of beech, ash, birch, whitebeam and field maple. This process (i.e. the thinning of the conifer content) has been very much in evidence recently, with large areas of the wood out of bounds to visitors due to woodland operations. Its effect is evident to all habitual visitors, with the originally dense woodland now looking almost sparse. Considering that the total number of trees there was in excess of 100,000, the scale of this work is significant, and has caused some concern locally from lay bystanders like myself, whose first reaction was: "hold on, you're destroying the wildlife cover!"

Nick Hazlitt helped to pacify this reaction, when I learnt that all this thinning out was in fact aimed at improving the wildlife cover, since the closely growing existing trees, mainly conifers and in excess of 60ft high, tended to result in the opposite.

Another reason for the recent assault on West Wood has been the policy of promoting biodiversity, which in simple terms means preventing the diminution of species and habitats which are in danger of disappearing. The more obvious examples of local endangered species are the dartford warbler, the nightingale and the dormouse, to mention but a few. Achieving this relatively new objective has entailed the removal and/or control of plants and wildlife which are posing a threat to it.

The commercial operations on all land owned or leased by the Forestry Commission are managed by Forest Enterprise, whose income very approximately derives from the following activities:

$1/3^{rd}$ from timber related activities

$1/3^{rd}$ from lettings and leasings

$1/3^{rd}$ from visitor centres, shops and film rights.

An example of the last item quoted was the film *Gladiator* made at their Farnham site. There is also income from woodland car parking fees, and leasing sites for charcoal burners. Providing open air recreation for the public ranks high in Nick Hazlitt's view of his functions, and he mentioned work done by the social research group Forest Research to establish the health benefits of woodland walking. These, although self-evident to enthusiasts such as myself, have been investigated and are listed in their recent publication under the title 'Trees and Woodlands – Nature's Health Service'. Amongst learned sources quoted are the Department of Health, Lancaster University, and various articles published in, for example, the *Journal of Environmental Psychology*.

We discussed also focal points of interest to promote these activities, such as erecting boards showing the location and history of the Sparsholt Roman villa, and landscaping of the forestry road approach to the site of the villa. These matters, I was informed, are all on-going. It's just a question of watching this space.

Apart from the Forestry Commission, there are other significant 'squatters' in West Wood: the wildlife. The resident squatters consist mainly of three species of deer, roe, fallow and muntjac, in addition to badgers and grey squirrels. The term 'squatting' in this context may be a slight misnomer, since this activity is permanent, and could be argued to be akin to having taken 'adverse possession' (a term that has recently surfaced in the consciousness of Sparsholt parishioners, as explained in Part 7 on Access). Wildlife squatters can also take adverse possession, without bothering to post notices of their intentions to take up residence

One of the most numerous mammal squatters, though seldom seen, are the muntjac deer. They were introduced into this country via the Duke of Bedford's estate at Woburn Abbey around 1894, and the current spread to most parts of England is attributable to escapees from there and subsequently also from Whipsnade Zoo. The Chinese muntjac, which these were, originally came from South-East Asia. They are prolific breeders, with their numbers having increased from around

5000 in 1950 to an estimated figure of between 40,000 and 100,000 today, out of a total deer population in England alone of in excess of 300,000[5]. Muntjac deer are not often seen, since they are relatively shy in addition to being a lot smaller than most other deer, smaller than a golden retriever in fact. They are also the oldest known deer species, going back to prehistoric times. In spite of their reputed shyness, there have been reports of them foraging around the town centre in Thetford, Norfolk, presumably under cover of darkness.

Muntjac are squat bodied and short antlered, and enjoy munching everything within their reach, including poisonous yew leaves, berries and dogs mercury, in fact practically all low-growing vegetation which is the principal habitat of native birds such as the nightingale, black cap and willow warbler. They also enjoy munching bramble thickets harbouring butterflies, as well as bluebells, orchids and fruit buds.

These traits, coupled with the fecundity of the species – the doe being virtually always pregnant after first going into season, have not endeared the muntjac to either the Forestry Commission in general or, in Sparsholt, the manager of Farley Mount Country Park (which includes the Crabwood Nature Reserve). Nationwide there is no closed season for their culling. Like the descendants of other immigrants in our midst, however, we should accommodate them in a humane (or mammalian?) manner, particularly bearing in mind that they did not force themselves on us like some older invaders such as the Danes and Normans.

Foxes are the only native predators on muntjac, and only fawns at that. Dogs are also known to be involved with killing adult muntjac, although these can defend themselves with their sharp incisors and have even been known to injure humans. A further consideration has to be the increasing likelihood of road accidents involving them. Even though small, a 35lb weight muntjac hitting a car doing 50mph can do significant damage. Although deer were implicated in some 20 human fatalities in 2008, it is not known how many of these involved muntjac.

Culling would therefore be the obvious answer, but this has to be hedged in by legislation to safeguard both the deer population and the public. A more radical approach suggested by the Mammal Society has been to re-introduce the lynx, reputedly native here until Roman times, and known to be a predator of small deer. There has even been a suggestion from Oslo University that wolves might be re-introduced in the Scottish Highlands to keep down the 400,000 red deer population there. At the time of writing a major Scottish landowner has announced plans to create a 9,000ha wildlife reserve incorporating both lynx and wolves, though enclosed by an 8ft high electrified fence. The idea of having these predators loose in Crab Wood might just create opposition from dog-owners or even those of us of a more nervous disposition. It would certainly make walkers think twice about letting their dogs off the lead!

To answer my questions regarding current deer culling methods I turned to the Forestry Commission's wildlife ranger for our area. His name cannot be revealed here, for fear of making him a target for extremist animal rights activists. I can say, however, that he must be every boy's idea of a traditional deer stalker, even apart from his hat which is just that (i.e. a deerstalker!). A genial character who has been active in deer management most of his life, some of it in Scotland, he was able to put me right on a number of points.

His last annual score in West Wood was 20 deer, with only one or two muntjac amongst them. The safety aspects of culling consist of shooting only from a vantage point from where, if the target is missed, the bullets will go 'to ground', i.e. in front of rising ground or from a shooting platform. In answer to my question why I had never seen such a platform in West Wood, he informed me that he carries it with him. Now the platforms I am familiar with would require a veritable giant to carry on his person, but modern technology has come up with a lightweight extendable solution, enabling it to be erected anywhere at short notice.

Armed with a 0.24 inch rifle, which is lethal at a range of 3500 yards (no metric concessions here!) the prey is normally shot at a range of between 20 and 80 yards. The bullet, I was informed, will go right though the deer, which will normally expire due to asphyxiation caused by loss of blood pressure. So what happens with the carcass? It goes straight to the Forestry Commission's refrigerated store, and then on to the butcher/retailer. There is, however, little financial incentive for the production of muntjac venison due to the small size and relatively high labour content of preparing the meat. It is worth noting, however, that this is rated highly amongst connoisseurs and widely eaten in China.

And where could I obtain some of this home-grown produce? Well, any local supermarket, but the only clue to origin would be the Forestry Commission logo. Most venison on sale would be from farmed herds, although the meat from these is in his opinion less acceptable because unlike deer shot in the wild it will have been affected by 'abattoir stress'. As for the type of deer, these are not normally identified on the packaging, but muntjac are not such a popular variety with the processors because they are very difficult to skin, almost as though the skin had been glued on.

More recent immigrants to Sparsholt are buzzards, which can now be seen circling on the thermals in pairs over West Wood in the summer months, and heard as well, with their characteristic short mournful cry. They have been spreading westward from Wales over the past few years, with reports of their overall numbers having more than doubled. They are the largest local bird of prey, with a wingspan of over 4ft (1.22m), and feed on anything available including voles, rabbits, birds, reptiles, insects and worms. I have even heard a local report of partridges being taken by them.

One of the most aerodynamically perfect of our birds of prey, they can glide for minutes at a time without flapping their wings, usually in pairs occasionally calling out to each other. Alerted by their cry, I have watched them soaring over West Wood, sometimes harried by a posse of rooks or seagulls worried about their young, only to outdistance them with a few disdainful flaps of their broad wings.

To what, if any, extent is the Forestry Commission assisted from the public purse? As far as I can gather, only to the extent that they were given a lot of land by the Government a long time ago. Some of this still belongs to us, though how much is impossible to ascertain due to the secrecy shrouding the Commission's land transactions. On the plus side we have to take into account the effect of trees in helping us reduce CO_2 emissions and thus combat global warming. But how can we put a price on that? And more relevant, how much of this benefit have we lost in the short term due to the drastic thinning in Westwood?

Over the years I have walked the forestry tracks through West Wood many times. As a result of my upbringing, I am imbued with an almost primeval belief that woods are my native habitat. My boyhood heroes were all woodlanders from way back, ranging from 'The Last of the Mohicans' to 'Leatherstocking' all mixed up with Robin Hood and tales of Sherwood forest. So any collection of trees brings to mind stalking Indians or the Sheriff of Nottingham's men.

In West Wood unfortunately there are few forest glades apart from a few open spaces created by the intersection of tracks or the existence of mounds where the sun has sufficient access to promote growth of wild flowers and shrubs. These would have helped to provide some additional interest to walkers whose appetite for looking at trees has become jaded, a likely consideration since a very approximate calculation shows the total tree population of West Wood, at least before the current massive thinning operation started, to be in the order of 100,000 to 200,000.

This is spread over some 260 ha (640 acres) incorporating a considerable variety of conifers and deciduous trees, interspersed by numerous green lanes, bridleways, forestry roads, wayfaring trails, footpaths and (as of quite recent origin) a BOAT (Byeway Open to All Traffic) but subject to a motorised vehicle traffic restriction order. The Forestry Commission has given unrestricted access to the public, subject to local and temporary closures for forestry operations. It is therefore widely patronised, mostly from car parks provided in the adjacent Farley Mount Country Park. It can be used for circular walks lasting up to about one hour, mainly through woodland, with some distant views at the northern and eastern fringe.

On the negative side, there are few places to sit, relax and enjoy just being there. There are no picnic sites, or even open spaces or glades, with the exception of one or two bridleway intersections and the site of the excavations for the Roman villa, which is still a fairly open space but already encroached on by the surrounding woodland. It is not marked in any way, and I believe I am one of only a handful of people who know the significance of the rapidly disappearing clearing. Some may say it is better left that way, but then this could be applied to every piece of our national heritage. Apart from the site of the Roman villa, there are other features of archaeological interest in West Wood, two sizeable tumuli, which also have no signboards explaining their origin.

For those willing to come early or late in the day, there is always a chance of deer sightings. West Wood also has opportunities for joggers and orienteering activities, and is without doubt a boon for those visitors from the nearby conurbations of Winchester and even Southampton who value fresh air and out-door activities, or even just exercising their dogs.

Complying with international agreements on biodiversity may be somewhat remote from our immediate environmental concerns. Like global warming, however, it will undoubtedly have a very marked effect on the lives of our children, and indeed the future of our species on this planet, if the experts are to be believed. Putting up with the temporary 'denuding' of West Wood should be seen as a very modest investment in the future. As part of a national enterprise aimed at sustaining our 'breathing' environment by combating the increase in CO2 emissions, we have every reason to continue to support the Forestry Commission, subject only to making it accountable for its activities, both locally and nationally. With the total land area in its possession in Britain estimated at over a million hectares, i.e. two and a half times the size of Hampshire, and believe it or not belonging to (or leased) by 'us', you could say that 'we' have a right to know what it is up to.

3.2 The County Council

Crab Wood was acquired by Hampshire County Council in 1967, and forms part of Farley Mount Country Park which comprises in addition Pitt Down, Farley Mount Monument and West Wood (owned by the Forestry Commission, as described above). A part of it is a Nature Reserve which encompasses a total area of 81 ha and is designated a site of Special Scientific Interest. The area lying on the eastern side of the road from Sparsholt to Standon incorporates recreational facilities such as a shelter with barbecue and playing fields.

Crab Wood is described by Hampshire County Council's Countryside Service as consisting of broadleaved woodland, hazel coppice with oak/ash overstorey, and being rich in scarce woodland flowers. It is managed as a part of its Recreation and Heritage Department by David Ball, the Farley Mount Country Park site manager. His post was once known as that of the 'Park Ranger' which had conjured up images of the Wild West as embodied by the Lone Ranger, involving horses and Stetsons, which is one that David Ball would, I conjecture, not be keen on being associated with. Although parts of his domain can resemble the Wild West, and although he does sometimes 'range' across it, neither horses, cows nor Stetsons are involved.

With a farming background David Ball is no stranger to the land, which is just as well, since Danebury Hill fort near Stockbridge, one of the 14 sites he is responsible for, has acquired a flock of sheep to maintain its chalk turf. But he see his primary activities and responsibilities, within the policy of the County Council's Country Park, as maintaining the wildlife richness (biodiversity) of the site together with its archaeological interest whilst facilitating the access enjoyed by the public. This means maintaining the current activities of coppicing i.e. harvesting of smaller growth, mainly hazel, to stimulate new growth to provide wildlife habitat), tree felling and ride management to create a diverse woodland habitat.

On the subject of coppicing, I am privileged to live in a cottage once occupied by one Bob Avery, who was a true 'woodman'. Perhaps the local 'Woodman Lane' and what used to be 'The Woodman' pub down the road from our cottage were named after an occupation carried on here for many years. Bob Avery leased coppicing rights in Crab Wood. His interest was not biodiversity but just earning a living out of making and selling hurdles, wattle fencing and bean poles out of the coppiced hazel shoots, and he was undoubtedly skilled at cutting back the smaller shoots in a way to encourage rapid re-growth. Some of the 'mature' locals remember occasionally giving him a hand getting his loaded cart up the slope from Woodman Lane to the cottage.

On the archaeological side David Ball has plans to erect

information boards explaining features such as the Roman Road, the Monument, the tumulus and medieval woodbanks, and the historical relationship of the area to the Royal Forest of West Bere. On the question of the conical depressions looking not totally unlike bomb caters in Crabwood, and my suggestion that they might be 'natural hollows' of the type prevalent in some parts of Dorset, he remained non-committal.

The woodland management policy will maintain the current activities of coppicing, tree felling and ride cutting to create a diverse woodland habitat. Much of Crab Wood was historically managed as hazel coppice, the harvesting of small poles from the stools cut every 7 years. This would have provided materials for hurdle making, house building, hedging and firewood. David Ball aims to continue this ancient practice although nowadays the coppice material is used in-house as well as providing material for local coppice craftsmen and also some Winchester allotments. A lot of the coppicing is actually carried out by outside volunteers such as the 'Wednesday Conservation Volunteers' (not only aimed at conserving Wednesdays) and students from Sparsholt College.

Wandering through the Crab Wood Nature Reserve brings home the age of some of the trees found there, many more than 200 years old and no longer considered saleable as timber. The abundant oaks are possibly from Victorian plantings and are of average quality, whilst the mixed coppice stools could be hundreds of years old and relics of the medieval coppice regime. The commercial value of the timber is at present extremely low due to competition from the unsustainable harvesting of tropical rain and northern conifer forests from the Baltic States.

In view of the very small number of crab trees to be found in Crab Wood, the name could be accounted for in two ways: Either the original number of crabs has very much reduced due to past management or lack of it, or the name was based on the fact that the timber there was 'crabby', i.e. of poor quality.

The wildlife in Crab Wood and the adjacent West Wood, apart from the usual species of birds common to this part of the world, consists of the fallow, roe and muntjac deer (already mentioned in connection with the Forestry Commission above), badgers, various bat species, and other small mammals. One of the more unusual of the latter species is the dormouse, also found on the adjacent Ham Green Common. Although dormouse breeding boxes have been installed, David Ball fears that increased public access has resulted in these boxes being disturbed with a resulting decline in their use.

In recent years coppicing in Crab Wood has been threatened by browsing of the increasing deer population. In particular, the coppice re-growth and ground flora have been heavily grazed by muntjac, to the extent that cessation of coppicing has been considered. The resulting loss of structural diversity and possible species decline however makes this option unacceptable for the present. It would in any case have a negative effect on English Nature's favourable Condition Assessment as a Site of Special Scientific Interest, quite apart from going against the precedent set by Hampshire County Council, the Forestry Commission and other bodies in trying to promote the continuity and re-instatement of coppice management across the wider landscape. The only other option would be through the control of the deer population by culling, which is currently still under discussion with the Forestry Commission.

A major current project aimed at protection of the coppice areas is the erection of deer fencing and assessing the relative cost and viability of four different types, most of which will only remain on site until such time as the renewed coppice re-growth has reached above 1.2metres, i.e. beyond the reach of browsing deer. This approach would allow Crab Wood to become a unique site where the different fencing options can be seen in operation. Together with management records of the time and biological data on coppice quality and ground flora, the site is then expected to become an extremely useful tool to illustrate the pros and cons of each fencing option. Their assessment will be enhanced by comparison with coppices left unfenced and only protected with lopped or dead hedging.

On the question of visitor numbers, David Ball said he had heard a figure for Farley Mount Country Park of up to 600,000 visitors per annum, though he thought this was probably on the high side. A quick spot check on my part at what I considered a peak attendance time of 1pm on a warm and bright August Bank Holiday weekend yielded a total number of 80 cars distributed over the all the available car parks. Assuming an average occupancy of 3 and an average stay of 1½ hours over a 7½ hour day, this implied a total visitor number for that day of 1200, so even in the highly unlikely event of this being replicated over all 365 days of the year it would still have only amounted to 438,000. On the other hand, with the population in the South continuing to increase, there is every reason to think that so will the visitor numbers in the Country Parks.

This then raises the costs of cleaning up after the multitude have left, and dealing with the effects of vandalism at the barbecue shelter in Crab Wood. Unfortunately, even litter alone poses a significant problem. I spent half an hour walking around the park after the main influx was over, and managed to fill up a garden sack with tins, bottles plastic bags and even the end results of 'poopa-scoops' neatly wrapped in plastic bags and left hanging on shrubs as decoration. Whether this indicates a perverted sense of humour or a terminal lassitude affecting the poop scooper after his heroic effort I have been unable to determine, since (fortunately, you might say) I do not number one in my acquaintanceship.

This is all part of our throw-away culture, which does raise the question as to whether we have the balance between freedom and responsibility right. A recent visit to Singapore brought home this question with graphic clarity. There, just depositing chewing gum on the side walk can result in significant fines and/or a visit to jail. Net result: spotless sidewalks.

But even if we had similar draconian regulations, the cost of appointing wardens to police these would be unacceptable. In the end our only hope lies in educating people to respect the rights of others – in this instance the rights of others to enjoy a countryside free from rubbish. In the meantime, and for those of us that care, there is always something we can do: take a garden sack along on our walks – after all, we own the place!

What we pay and what we get
The annual budget of the Hampshire's Countryside Service is

around £6 million, which works out at nearly £5 per head of Hampshire's population. The Crab Wood part of the Country Park harbours a mass of bluebells in the spring, with lots of footpaths and bridleways criss-crossing the area, and is an ideal venue for circular walks of up to ¾ hours, some of these through quite ancient woodland with huge beeches together with views out across the Hampshire countryside from the northern fringe of the Crab Wood nature reserve, with always a chance of sighting deer or other wildlife. There are in addition several open spaces large enough for the children to play football on, together with a barbecue shelter adjacent to the Crab Wood car park.

3.3 Sparsholt College

In 1914 Hampshire County Council set up a Farm School at the present site in Sparsholt. During the Second World War it was known as the Sparsholt Farm Institute, and made a considerable contribution to the war effort by training recruits for the Women's Land Army to enable them to take over farming work from men conscripted to fight in the war. After the war the Institute became Sparsholt Agricultural College. With 176 ha (437 acres), it is the second largest public landowner in the parish. It's public in the sense that it's funded by the government as a college of further education, incorporated as a trust run by a board of governors who are responsible to the LSC (Learning and Skills Council).

In accordance with its mission statement it is 'the local, regional and major national centre of excellence for education and training in the provision of learning and skills to the land based and rural sector community'. Quite a mouthful, and the term 'land-based' is of considerable importance, as will be seen below. Its full implication came as somewhat of surprise to me, since I had blithely assumed that the college was there to teach prospective farmers to plough, sow, reap and milk the cows. Although this is still true for some of the curriculum, the greater part is now taken up by courses not directly related to farming.

Tim Jackson, the principal, filled me in on the various activities going on at the College, now incidentally no longer known as "Sparsholt Agricultural College" but as "Sparsholt College Hampshire". Amongst the various courses not directly related to farming are: Animal Management & Veterinary Nursing, Engineering, Fishery Studies, Game Wildlife and Countryside Studies, Equine Studies, Horticulture, Forestry & Arboriculture, Sport Outdoor Education and Uniformed Services, Health and Safety and, last but not least, Services to Business. Enough, one might think, to be getting on with. But there was more to come. With the recent acquisition of Cricklade College in Andover, Tim Jackson is now in addition responsible for courses there, which also encompass hairdressing. So what is even remotely land-based about hairdressing? Simple: even farmers need to have their hair cut occasionally!

Tim Jackson is therefore now at the helm of an undertaking accounting for a turnover in excess of £25 million, with more than 2500 students to tend to. By demeanour he is the very antithesis of somebody like Sir Alan Sugar, certainly not likely to say 'You're fired' to anybody, at least not in Sir Alan's manner. He occupies a modest office overlooking the Sparsholt College Campus, although now spending more of his time at the Andover College to supervise the re-organisation there. If he should have any vaulting ambitions, these would no doubt be curbed by the supervisory board, of which he is a member. This consists of 17 members in total, two members of staff, two student members (both lots elected), plus the Chairman and other members appointed by Hampshire County Council, and the National Farmers Union. All very democratic and representative, but the mind does boggle at how this motley assortment can come up with anything coherent as a result of their deliberations. Presumably they do, since the College has been functioning for a number of years.

The reason for moving away from purely agricultural courses is simple: there was not much money to be made in agriculture. The customer for food products (i.e. us) is principally interested in paying as little as possible for them in order to leave money to be spent on more important items such as computer games for the children or garden ponds and associated fountains and water features, which can quickly add two decimal points to one's credit card account (so Tim Jackson ruefully confessed).

This may be the reason for Fishery Studies now being on the curriculum. More up-market are 'Equine Studies' to serve people who can afford to keep horses for the children, sometimes even for themselves. To provide further entertainment for the little ones it is now possible to acquire exotic animals and insects, ranging from snakes and lizards to scorpions. All these need knowledge in handling for the businesses concerned, and this is where the college scores. Keeping wildlife confined to the campus can give rise to the occasional call from a local resident about a strange animal in their garden. 'Not a sabre toothed tiger, or a Boa constrictor perhaps?' I ventured hopefully. 'No, they don't keep those,' Tim Jackson told me, 'but there was the case of a Mara (this is of course a rodent which looks like a cross between a rabbit and a small deer)' spotted by a mystified local resident in his garden.

Other animals resident on the college land include a variety of small mammals, amphibians and birds, and extend to more exotic species like wallabies, monkeys, llamas, alpacas and scorpions. This still leaves the rearing of native wild birds such as pheasants, partridges and even stone curlews, together with a fish hatchery and a one hectare fishing lake stocked with bream, carp and trout amongst many others.

Tim Jackson has been at the College since 1986, becoming principal in 1998. During his term 'in office' he has had to weather the foot-and-mouth outbreak in 2000. On one occasion he was returning from a business trip to find the college entrance under police guard, threatening him with arrest if he attempted to return to his home on the campus. He eventually persuaded the man in charge to let him through on the understanding he would not leave the campus for the duration. He also negotiated passage for his wife, who had been sitting in a car park in Winchester wondering what to do. So there are perks with the job.

Apart from escaping wildlife and the ever present threat of foot-and-mouth, there is the occasional brush with villagers who have been the victim of a prank during the annual 'student rag', sometimes resulting in temporary or even permanent loss of house signs. Students will be students, you might say. And so will irate home-owners. The village pub has in any case banned students from their premises, which are more attuned to up-market eaters than student drinkers. There are of course club facilities on campus where the drinking age is strictly controlled, and there is another pub on the fringe of the parish down the road from the college.

Permanent residents on the college land now make up a total human complement of about 1500 during term time, thus adding considerably to the parish population. Their impact on the rest of the parish residents is, however, minimal, primarily because, apart from a narrow country lane with rather widely spaced overtaking places, the main access road to the college is from the main road which also serves the village. This contributes to some isolation from the village community, which is exacerbated by the fact that the college provides its own recreational amenities, and the village pub, shop and post office are in any case too difficult to access for students without their own transport.

During the annual 'Open Days' the college attracts visitors from a wide radius to display its multifarious activities, thus also giving villagers a chance find out what they get up to at the college.

To provide back-up for the traditional agricultural courses, the college incorporates a working farm which takes up the bulk of the college land. Graham Boyt, the Farm Manager, filled me in on the extent of his empire, which consists of some 300 head of dairy/beef cattle, 2000 pigs, 300 sheep, 60 horses and a 40 head herd of Sika deer, not to mention the students. In addition to the livestock farm, arable crops including maize, grass for silage and winter wheat are grown.

Graham Boyt got his NDA (National Diploma in Agriculture)

5a   College Principal Tim Jackson: no Sir Alan Sugar

5b   and Farm Manager Graham Boyt: hands on

6   Beyond the pale? eco-friendly village home

at Stroud, and came to Sparhsolt College in 1989, initially as a tractor driver. After a meteoric rise 'through the ranks' (not I suspect an appropriate term on the land), he became Farm Manager in 1990. He reports to the head of Finance, no doubt since his activities make a considerable contribution to the college coffers. The biggest money earner is sheep, because of the small labour content. Then come pigs, and finally, in a near break-even situation, the dairy, although this might improve after recent negotiations with the supermarkets. The figures for annual output he quoted off the cuff were impressive: 30 tons of beef, 184 tons of bacon, 20 tons of lamb and 1.2 million litres of milk. – and all this with a total staff complement of 3 full-times and 3 part timers directly responsible to him. In addition to managing the farm, he spends the remainder of his time giving practical demonstrations to students and supervises the repair of machinery damaged by them in the process, in addition to filling in forms for DEFRA. In 1989 he had 11 staff and 13 tractors for 180 agricultural students. This has shrunk to 2 tractors and 40 students.

It's a 60 hour week for Graham Boyt, and he is committed to the open air life. A particular reward of his job is seeing handicapped children acquire skills to enable them to live a useful life. But his own children are unlikely to follow in his footsteps. They see a more remunerative future in information technology, with a starting rate of around 30k for a normal 37hour week.

So what about the future for farming? If he owned a farm, he would go for a 'Farm Theme Park' type of visitor attraction. Certainly livestock farming is likely to remain in the doldrums, though arable farming is about to revive with the growing demand for bio-fuel crops and a worldwide shortfall in wheat.

3.4 The Parish Council

Ask not what you can do for your parish, ask what it can do for you. This might appear a pretty cynical statement, but I suspect it applies, even if only subconsciously, to the great majority of country dwellers. Much as we might sneer at what are often co-opted councillors, or ones re-elected on a nod and a wink, they still do more than most of us for the parish, if only by giving up their spare time to attend meetings.

Sparsholt Parish Council does not figure in the big league when it comes to the control of land. In order of size, it has dominion over Ham Green Common, the village playground, and the Well House (see 'Post Office' below), all in all about four hectares. I say 'dominion over' advisedly, since this is based on hearsay, and I have not dared to check it by following up the various deeds involved, which would have taken me and a team of researchers another century I can ill afford. Let's just assume that the parishioners' first port of call for any questions relating to the parish land holdings would be the Parish Council.

Before investigating what the PC does with these munificent hectares under its control it is advisable to have a look at what the Parish Council is there for, and what it does when not engaged in administering its landholdings. It certainly was advisable in my case, since my profound ignorance regarding local government quickly became apparent.

A look at the internet came up with some fascinating

snippets. Amongst others, it informs us that there are around 10,000 community, parish and town councils in England and Wales, and 100,000 councillors. Furthermore, these councils have a large range of powers, and the activities they are involved in are immense.

This came as a surprise to me, and, I venture to guess, would also come as such to the councillors involved, certainly as regards their large range of powers. Perhaps it might have been better to keep quiet about that – who knows what they might get up to if they find out. Are they also aware, I asked myself, that they are, or should be, involved in planning, promoting tourism, licensing, community halls, representation (of what?) and management of village centres?

To put an end to these conjectures I plucked up courage and approached an ex councillor with between 16 and 20 years (he has lost count) of service under his belt, or wherever he keeps them. John Steel, as it happens, has not only been a parish councillor, but also a Winchester City councillor, and, for three years, leader of Winchester City Council, followed by a spell as Mayor, some concurrent with his position of parish councillor. When it comes to local government experience, I had certainly hit the jackpot, and, as it turned out, the horse's mouth I had been looking for. Not only that, but someone whose long-standing service to the community entitles him to be looked up to. In his case, I should add it is necessary to do so at all times if you happen to be less than six feet tall.

He patiently explained what his responsibilities as parish councillor had amounted to, and although he was not able to throw any light on the promotion of mass tourism to Sparsholt, he did confirm that councillors are there to help parishioners if at all possible. The Parish Council also provides a venue for residents to air their grievances, mostly to do with planning matters, which are normally guaranteed to boost public attendance at parish council meetings. In addition, it delegates councillors to sit on the School and Village Hall Committees in order to have a parish input to these venerable institutions, and arranges special functions such as the Millennium Celebration. This event is of course not likely to be repeated very frequently, and it would appear highly unlikely that any of us will be here for a repeat performance. But the parish does have something to remember it by: a commemorative painting showing an aerial view of the village at the time of the celebrations.

The Parish Council under its erstwhile Chairman David Stockwell, now sadly deceased, was also instrumental in the development of a housing association building venture which enabled younger residents engaged in setting up home to remain in the village. Since this required development of land outside the planning department housing envelope for the village, the housing association involved had to produce evidence of social needs in order to obtain planning permission.

Another Parish Council achievement involved the post office and the new playground. After closure of the previous village post office and shop, the parish arranged for premises known as 'The Well House' to be made available for this purpose at a peppercorn rent to an enterprising pair of ladies (see Post Office). When parents formed a playground association to bring the existing playground into the 21st century, the parish also came to their aid with advice and a subsidy to help it along.

It also worked together with the County Council in assisting in the formation of the 'Ham Green Conservation Volunteers', who give their time and labour to keep the Common eco-friendly.

All this may lead you to think that all is sweetness and light in the village, which would not be true to life. The above-mentioned housing development is now history, and no further affordable housing is in the pipeline. So what is it that gets the village excited? It's affordable housing, of course, or indeed any new developments. There should not have been any doubt that Sparsholt would be exempt from the nationwide problem of those living a privileged low-density existence in the country wanting to pull up the drawbridge. They become Nimbys. As a result, any parish meetings to do with planning matters are guaranteed to boost public attendances.

The recent history of Sparsholt will demonstrate why this should be so. It shows that those who were born here or who have been here a long time, are decreasing in numbers. Newcomers are infiltrating at an increasing pace. What used to be council properties have been sold off, and those who cannot afford to compete in the local housing market have to migrate to the larger estates. This means not just Winchester, which is a singularly high-cost area, but more likely Southampton or Portsmouth and their associated satellites, where social housing is still available.

All this amounts to the dispersal of families, which is reflected nationwide and has been happening at an increasing pace over the last five decades. It heralds the end of 'the village' as portrayed in our literature and the media, as a place where families have lived for generations. This may be a regrettable situation, but it is a fact of modern life. On the positive side, many of us, including myself, are in the village not because we have always been there, but because we chose to be there. We are privileged to have had this choice available to us, but not all of us think we should be prepared to give our less privileged fellow citizens an opportunity to share this privilege, and even those who do will mostly only contemplate new developments as long as they are not within hailing distance, and preferably not in sight.

This is of course precisely the issue where the division in the village becomes apparent. Village design statements have been presented and approved by the Parish Council, but do not make any provision for new development. A tentative discussion some years ago relating to a possible site for affordable housing met with considerable hostility from the owners of adjacent properties, not even aimed at specific layouts, but just the principle.

The net result is that newcomers from the lower-income occupations such as most nurses, teachers, policemen, social workers and others are excluded. Are they undesirable hoi-polloi? Or are we expelling not only many of the people who were born here, but also keeping out those who are able to provide the services we all need?

So far I have not mentioned business or industrial developments. Yet these would create some of the additional local employment needed to help reduce the amount of commuting. Since there are already many residents using their homes for carrying on a business, why not contemplate new businesses occupying their own premises?

Current thinking about reducing restrictions on green belt development may be the first inkling of recognition that in order to keep the village alive and functioning as a social entity as it was when its inhabitants worked on the land, we need to provide more employment right here. This will ensure the continuation of the social amenities provided by the school, the village hall and the shop-cum-post office. A parish of 1500 ha. can easily accommodate another 10 ha of business and/ or industrial premises without disastrous effect on the rural environment we have now. As with all new development in the countryside, it's not the principle which should be a matter for debate, but how it is done.

To what extent the village design plan is of benefit in this respect is a matter for debate. It says, for example, that the style and design of new buildings need not mimic existing buildings as long as they respect existing styles and materials. This does sound to me like a contradiction in terms. So what would happen if someone wanted to build an eco-friendly home made of timber and glass in Sparsholt with solar panels on the roof? Is this beyond the pale? And yet energy efficient houses may soon become a condition for getting planning permission. For the more traditionally inclined readers I would recommend not looking at illustration 6 showing just such a house in a (simulated) village setting.

And who are to be the arbiters of good taste in these matters? If the first cavemen in the area had been confronted with a wattle and thatch cottage, they would probably have decided that this was a totally unnatural and tasteless habitation and thrown a few rocks at it. After a few millennia of getting used to the smokeless comforts provided by the revolutionary new design, they would have abandoned the cave and moved into the wattle and thatch cottage. Needless to say, when brick and tiles came on the scene, there would have been revulsion, no doubt resulting in the occupiers of these atrocious new habitations getting a good dunking in the village pond. But lo and behold, a few centuries on, we've got used to the idea, though the purists might still hanker for the old wattle and thatch.

3.5   The Common

If you go down to the woods today you might just be in for a surprise – not a teddy bears' picnic but a happy band of parishioners (illustration 7a) chopping, sawing, cutting and burning the undergrowth on Ham Green Common, a strip of land not much wider than 90ft over most of its total length of just over half a mile, covering an area of 3.6 ha. It runs almost exactly east-west along what was once known as the Ox Drove, which was presumably used to supply the city of Winchester and others further to the west with beef and lamb from Wales.

This Common was first registered as 'an ownerless Common' by the Parish Council in 1976 (1) when it became apparent that no owner could be found. Perhaps it was another case of the venerable Dean and Chapter of Winchester either not finding the deeds amongst their records, or perhaps not being aware that this so called manorial waste was once attributed to having belonged to the Church. A local historian (Cecilia Knowles) found that all the land within seven leagues of the city (i.e. Winchester) was left to the Church by King Cynegils of Wessex, and who am I to question that? She also mentions the purchase of one acre of the Common by a local man from 'the lords of the manor', whoever they were, as recently as the 1880s.

I should hasten to explain that manorial waste in this context does not mean that the Common was ever a rubbish dump used by the lords of the manor. No and emphatically no. A quick forage on the internet led me immediately to the horse's mouth on the subject, that is of course the Planning Inspectorate, no less. And they did come up with a definition, albeit as with all governmental definitions, hedged with obfuscations. Let me illustrate: 'The definition normally relied upon is the one given in *Attorney General v Hanmer (1858),* namely "the open, uncultivated and unoccupied lands of the manor"'. The first two elements of this definition, the Planning Inspectorate go on to say, are self explanatory. When it comes to the third, i.e. 'unoccupied' (one can almost hear a sharp intake of breath) this is a grey area that has not been tested in the courts. Readers may be concerned to learn (or perhaps relieved) that this is not a problem which it is the duty of inspectors to resolve. Perhaps this implies that we, the parishioners, are on our own on this one.

However, have no fear, ye local commoners, Ham Green Common is registered as a common. In accordance with the law this entitles you, provided of course that you are a bona fide commoner, to 'take or use some portion of that which another man's land naturally produces'. All clear? Well, no. Not to worry, though, us don't knows are in good company. Let me quote DEFRA on the subject: 'In legal terms', it states, 'there is no single definition of the term "common land"'. After further deliberations on the uncertainty of the meaning, it goes on to hazard that 'perhaps the most transparent approach today is to consider common land to be all the land registered under the 1965 Act .....'. So if DEFRA aren't sure, what chance is there for us poor mortals?

Having been left somewhat obfuscated on the meaning of 'the Common', we are left further up the creek when trying to sort out what makes a 'commoner'. My dictionary defines him (or her of course, or maybe not) as being a person not belonging to the nobility, or without noble rank or title, or just one of the common people. In fact, just about the vast majority of 'us'. But what has that to do with commons and those who exercise the ancient rights of commoners? Simply that these commoners were originally people who owned no land but were granted access to other peoples' land over certain areas known as commons to graze cattle and collect wood. Nowadays it applies principally to people who have registered these rights, such as the Commoners in the New Forest, and who are thereby permitted to graze ponies and cattle on this land. The total amount of land registered as commons in England and Wales encompasses a considerable 2000 square miles, or 4% of the total land area.

So who are the commoners in Sparsholt? There are, in fact, none. The registration of Ham Green as a common simply means that it has free public access, and that its care and maintenance is the responsibility of the local community. And what can we remove from the common? Berries, perhaps, but not on an industrial scale. If there were any commoners left, they would find very little land suitable for horse grazing, or keeping pigs or sheep on for that matter, or removing dead wood for firewood, although that's what commoners were allowed to do in bygone ages.

The facts on the ground, appropriately, are that parishioners would have no interest in any of these activities, except perhaps the picking of sloes, which grow on Ham Green Common in abundance, and are good for making sloe gin. In addition, though not normally taking to grazing their animals, they do also use the common for walking their dogs, or even their spouses. The Common's main function as far as the villagers are concerned is thus in provide an open space with extensive views for walkers, riders and cyclists by means of both a footpath and a bridleway (once part of the Ox Drove mentioned above) through the common.

So who are those people in the chainsaw gang clearing the undergrowth? Why, they are of course that indefatigable crew of eco-warriors, the Ham Green Conservation Volunteers, formed in 2002, and committed to manage the Common for the benefit of wildlife, flora and fauna, and for the enjoyment of the local community. As is often the case, the formation and on-going success of this band of volunteers was due to the initiative of one person, in this case one Mike Johnn, an ex resident of Sparsholt who has since returned to his native South Africa. Apart from his personal help in carrying out the work, he was also instrumental in obtaining a grant of over £4000 from the Local Heritage Initiative.

The Volunteers give their spare time to help keep an equitable balance between the demands of weeds and ivy and other undesirable growth and those of wild flowers, butterflies, birds and mammals threatened with extinction if they don't get a helping hand (or chainsaw!). One of the endangered species, the dormouse, has even been provided with affordable accommodation by these champions of the environment, but in spite of this it is diminishing and a cause of concern.

The Volunteers are supported with equipment and insurance by Sparsholt Parish Council, and work under guidelines and advice given by the Hampshire and Isle of Wight Naturalist Trust. They also help in counting and reporting on the numbers and kinds of animal life and insects they encounter, which include butterflies, moths, dormice, yellow-necked mice and field voles, and carry out surveys of wild flowers and the various species of trees found on the Common.

On the wider scene the internet enables me to report that at a gathering of commoners and experts on commons at the University of Gloucestershire in 2007, it was stated that there are 2000 square miles of registered common land in England and Wales, representing around 4% of the land area. If this be so, then Sparsholt parish is lagging behind with a mere 2.8%. I have an idea of how this inequity can be rectified, but more of that in Part 7 dealing with access.

3.6 The Playground

The playground today consists of several parts: the Kiddies playground, the football pitch and a basketball pitch together with a grassed area for other ball games, together occupying approximately a quarter hectare of ground bounded by the original council estate road dating back to the time when the houses were mainly occupied by council tenants.

The original playground was about one quarter of its present size and sported a single swing and a kiddies' slide, until Wendy Dean and Liz West (illustration 7b) hit the village

7a   The common with happy band

7b   The playground with movers and shakers Wendy Dean (left) and
Liz West

A cut above...Farley Mount's remaining yews after their short-back-and-sides TC60/87/30

County defends yew felling

A Bishop's Waltham nature-lover has blasted Hampshire County Council for axeing seven yews around Farley Mount and making the rest look "like palm trees".

Joyce Thatcher said she was incensed with the sight on Mount Down at the beauty spot near Winchester. "It's disgusting. I went up there with my grandchildren and I couldn't believe it.

by Ali Kefford

"They've chopped down some and the others have been cut right back. They're now standing like palm trees.

"I do love walking there with the dogs. In other parts of the country they look after their yew trees. I just hope they know what they're doing. I thought they could have done something to underpin the monument."

Ranger, Graham Long,

who runs the Farley Mount Country Park on behalf of the county, said the 35-foot high trees were cut down because they were casting a shadow over the grass and killing it.

He explained that, as a result, rains were washing away the soil and undermining the steeple-shaped monument. "We had to do something, or it could have toppled over," said Mr Long.

"There are now four nice yews evenly spaced. Every-

one has said how much nicer it looks. We've had loads of compliments. It was a tangled mess before."

The monument is to a horse called "Beware Chalk Pit". In 1733, the game steed leapt into a 25-foot deep chalkpit with owner, Paulet St John, on his back. Next year, he won the Hunters' Plate on Worthy Downs.

Mr St John's black stone memorial slab, is in nearby Farley Chamberlayne church.

8   Farley Mount onslaught: no consultation

around 1998. They both had children who needed something more exciting to entertain them, and they were determined to see that they got it. Wendy took the matter up with the Parish Council, and managed to get the approval of the Committee, and for the playground as well! As a result, Wendy and Liz formed the Sparsholt Playground Association, roping in John Steel, the then local city councillor (and later Mayor of Winchester) amongst others to become trustees and eventually occasional part time gardeners to boot.

Wendy badgered Hampshire County Council, the Parish Council, the Lottery Fund and the Hampshire Playing Fields Association until she got what they needed – a mere £40,000. This provided them with the landscaping, fencing and up-to-date playground equipment, though still leaving annual insurance, maintenance costs, lease and inspection costs to be met.

At the end of all this, we have a landscaped playground incorporating a swing, a log roll, a tightrope walk, a climbing frame and the challenging Gyro-Spiral, which is of course a form of rotating see-saw, not to mention the football, cricket and basketball pitches.

The insurance alone amounts to around £1000 pa – a bit of an eyebrow raiser, but then they have to cover themselves for parental claims from an increasingly litigious society. Safety in playgrounds is in any event subject to strict scrutiny, with annual inspections obligatory. According to the RoSPA (The Royal Society for the Prevention of Accidents) there are currently some 40,000 hospitalisations annually resulting from playground accidents. Although this figure is considerably lower than that for accidents in the home, one wonders how it squares up with the vociferous media comments on the overprotective Nanny State, and whether it begs the question of who decides if and when this figure is low enough to warrant some correction. Perhaps we should be prepared to accept a higher number of hospitalisations!

The IIRSM (International Institute of Risk and Safety Management, of course) holds, and I quote, that 'modern playgrounds are safer now than they were 35 years ago. They do not need fall heights of over four metres or concrete surfaces to be exciting for children.' But should the Minister for Health and Safety (Lord Whatshisname) see to it that the little blighters learn about risk the hard way, and have all those climbing frame bases in concrete, as they used to be in the 'hard old days'?

Food for thought here. Perhaps the State Nanny, Lord Whatshisname, should be pensioned off, and replaced by a Minister for Risk and Enterprise, in order to correct excessive coddling. He might go further than playgrounds and also prohibit the wearing of car seat belts. No doubt there'll be objections when the extra trillion is needed by the NHS to cope, but this might turn out to be a temporary blip as the resulting increase in fatalities will lead to a corresponding reduction in the demand on the NHS. The effects on business could also be beneficial, with undertakers in particular making a killing, as one might put it. In addition this would also give more employment to that sector of the legal profession dealing with claims from a rapidly escalating number of surviving dependants.

I could go on, but it's time to return to earth and the Sparsholt playground. This, in its current version, has now been in operation since 2001 and no fatalities have been reported, nor any claims for £3 million in compensation for a finger that got lost after being stuck in the wrong position at the wrong time, or a head for the same reason, and long may this boring state of affairs continue. The original movers and shakers, their children now old enough to find more adult entertainment, are retiring from the Playground Association, whose functions will be taken over by the Parish Council.

3.7 Where we have our say

There appears to be an assumption that in the case of public landowners, we don't need to have a say because we are the owners anyway, and our appointed representatives will ensure that all is done for our best. In real life, this has not invariably been so, and it behoves us all to keep an eye on what our supposed servants are doing with our land.

When it comes to gleaning information, my experience of dealing directly with public servants, both in national and in local government, has been wide and varied. Merely to impress on them that they are supposed to be our (and my) servants has been a problem. This may be because on average, their take home remuneration is considerably more than most of us aspire to, and they would therefore not be impressed by being told that it's my modest tax contribution (huge in my eyes) that's helping them to stock up on caviar.

Although generally prepared to listen, the common immediate reaction of public servants to requests for information is to refer one to the relevant internet web page. Where the request relates to public expenditure or staffing, it usually creates an immediate defensive knee-jerk reaction invariably resulting in a falling back on to the Data Protection Act, leaving the petitioner to fall back on the Freedom of Information Act as a last resort. It then becomes apparent that the two are often contradictory. Another variation on this theme is, yes, the information can be supplied, but would have to be charged for on a time basis. No actual figures are usually mentioned, possibly because the informant is banking on the petitioner not being willing to proceed down that road, which would normally be the case, bearing in mind that public servants are not known to be fast movers..

Putting forward suggestions at departmental levels regarding methods of operation or interpretations of national or local government policy, both by telephone and in writing, have usually met with a delayed if courteous response, but I cannot recall one instance where they have been acted upon. The overriding reaction is, yes, that would be a good idea, but we don't have the resources to do it.

Representations concerning local matters have already been dealt with under the heading of Parish Council. In addition to our parish and district councillors we are represented on our County Councils, or, in some areas of England and Wales, on Unitary or Metropolitan Councils. In the case of Sparsholt, we are represented on Hampshire County Council by a councillor who is responsible for five wards incorporating Sparsholt and deals with everything ranging from parish road re-surfacing, speed limit signs, childrens' and adult services, care packages, recreation and heritage, fuel poverty and energy action groups to footpaths and libraries, in addition to reporting to nine parish councils on grants available to them from the County Council or other governmental organisations such as DEFRA, or even the European Union.

It would appear, at least to me, that being a county councillor is not a particularly rewarding occupation unless one enjoys suffering for a good cause. On the basis of spending 35 hours or more a week attending committee meetings and dealing with constituents, they are paid for their time at a rate just about approaching the national minimum wage. In addition, they have to answer for their actions at public meetings to an often unappreciative and sometimes even abusive audience, though the latter is usually confined to one or two apoplectic individuals.

There are of course numerous topics affecting the land which are already being campaigned for by organisations such as Greenpeace, Friends of the Earth, The Wildlife Preservation Society, the RSPB, the Council for the Preservation of Rural England, English Heritage and many others. The most effective way of having one's say on the larger issues is to support one of these, though there is no harm in letting off steam on an individual basis in addition – it's all grist to the mill.

The interface between the local representatives of the Forestry Commission and the public is difficult to find. No doubt our local county councillor sitting on the Hampshire County Council Recreation and Heritage Committee would be able to relay any concerns such as the one raised above regarding the extent of tree felling in West Wood.

The view of our local forestry manager, Nick Hazlitt, was that although they would welcome good relations with the local populace, the Forestry Commission is mainly accountable to the wider community, which in some respects even extends to the global community. He quoted the 1992 Rio Agreement on Biodiversity (full name 'the Earth Summit's Convention on Biological Diversity') as an example. This was followed up in 1993 by the then UK Forestry Minister signing up to the General Guidelines for Sustainable Management of Forests and the Conservation of Biodiversity of European Forests.

The decisions then made on our behalf may not have caused much concern in Sparsholt at the time. In recent years, however, the felling of a good portion of West Wood did grab our attention. How this will affect biodiversity is a matter for the experts, and suffice to say these are agreed on the long term benefits in this respect.

In general, and within the framework of the aforesaid international agreements, Nick Hazlitt assured me that wherever possible the local community would be asked to comment on any proposed changes in the layout of West Wood. Conversely, he recently responded to a request from the Parish Council to put them in the picture regarding the Forestry Commission's activities in the Parish by contributing an account which was published in the Parish newsletter. He also mentioned plans to get local schools involved with their nearest forestry areas with a view to stimulating nature walks and a general interest in enjoying and maintaining these.

Beyond that there is no intention of any formal liaison with parishes which contain significant areas of Forestry Commission land, nor even to liaise with Hampshire County Council in providing information boards regarding the site of the Roman villa or the tumuli in the Forestry part of the Farley Mount Country Park.

Farley Mount Country park, including the Crab Wood nature reserve, is run by Hampshire County Council, although it includes the Forestry Commission land dealt with above. Since it is the responsibility of the Recreation and Heritage Department of Hampshire County Council, it could be argued that we have our say by virtue of being represented there by our county councillor.

My own experience in recent years has been that, as happened with West Wood, users were also faced with a *fait accompli* in Farley Mount Country park. I am referring here to a particular example pertaining to Farley Mount itself, which is actually just outside the Sparsholt Parish boundary, when most of the old trees around the Farley Mount Monument were felled, and many parents were saddened by the fact that their children were now deprived of the opportunity to play hide and seek in the shrubbery under the trees. Illustration 7 is a newspaper cutting dating from that time.

The reasons given were that the tree roots were undermining the mound. Whether this had in fact been sufficiently corroborated or not I do not know. Had there, however, been a user group in existence, I feel some reasonable compromise might well have been reached. The matter of setting up such a body was mooted, but the immediate reaction seemed to be that we don't really want to draw too much attention to the Country Park since it has enough visitors already.

In the case of Sparsholt College we are dealing with a Trust responsible to the Learning and Skills Council (LSC), described as a non-departmental publicly funded body with an annual budget of over £10 billion. Any input from the public would therefore have to be via the Principal of the College, and/or the Chairman of the Trust. In general, any such input would generally be concerned with student matters. However, since the College incorporates a sizeable chunk of land, some of it traversed by a public footpath, it could be argued there is a need for some regulated interchange between the College and the parish beyond the report about College activities presented annually at the Parish Council AGM by the College Principal. On the broader and more vexed question of access (see Part 8 below) the Hampshire County Council would have to be involved, via our county councillor.

When it comes to matters pertaining to the parish, our first point of contact would be through our parish councillors, each one of whom has a specific area of remit, ranging from: planning, school, footpaths and common, highways, environment, playground and transport to the village hall. Failing that, we have an opportunity to raise any issues during the public questions session at the monthly parish council meetings held at the village hall. This also applies to matters involving the Common and the playground, both of which are administered by the Parish Council.

Although the parish has some input on planning matters through the Village Design Plan, it is the City Council which sets out its policies for guiding the use and development of land and buildings within the Winchester district. Parishioners also have a say on this through their representation on this august body via their city councillor (one of 57), who is elected every four years for the ward of Sparsholt, which also includes another two adjacent parishes. Apart from planning matters, the City Council also deals with housing, environmental health, refuse collection, parks, museums etc.

Planning policies are in turn steered by county-wide policies, and a further tier of representation is introduced here through the county councillor for Sparsholt, which for this purpose belongs to the Downlands Division. This is mostly a political appointment, i.e with the councillor representing a party, with elections held every four years. The County Council also deals with planning matters, but only those falling within the following topics: infrastructure changes such as associated changes in road layouts, the release of reserve housing sites where applicable, and the control of mineral extraction, which has to be in accordance with the agreed County Mineral Plan. For the rest, the County Council is principally engaged on education and social services (particularly care of the elderly). It is in addition responsible for recycling and waste (no, not the local taxpayers' money), roads and transport, rights of way and libraries.

Finally we arrive at regional and national plans and policies, where we are represented by our MP.

The very involved tier structure governing local planning decisions illustrates how little input parishioners can have. Planning regulations are still governed by the 1990 Town and Country Planning Act which is currently under review. Its critics point out that planning restrictions relating to the Green Belt in particular have led to an acute housing shortage, soaring house prices, congested roads and 'identikit' developments. As far as local planning applications are concerned, parishioners have very little power, apart from appealing against the relevant planning officer's interpretation of the planning laws. And whatever happens, the Winchester District Local Plan shows a defined policy boundary, outside which new development will only be permitted where essential and generally only for agricultural purposes.

Part 4

The Yield

Looking at what grows on the land of Sparsholt brought home to me the origin of that time-honoured and Women's Institute beloved phrase 'This green and pleasant land' without necessarily any accompanying urge to build Jerusalem on it. In addition to the woodland which accounts for a quarter of the parish 'green' land, the grass accounts for 20%. Even this does not include the garden lawns, the playing fields or grass verges along the roads.

Nationwide the figure for grass coverage is even more impressive, with some 55% of the total land area covered in it. This difference between what happens in our parish and what happens nationwide can be partly accounted for by the type of grass defined in the National Agricultural Statistics as 'Sole right rough grazing', which means all grazing land on mountain, moor, heath and downland. This accounts for 18% nationwide, but is not present in Sparsholt.

In springtime the growing crops contribute to the 'greenness', as do the odd millions of lawns spread around the country. Though these add to the pleasantness of the environment, it has to be said that just keeping them in good trim must account for a good proportion of the CO_2 being belched up into the ozone layer.

Looking at grass purely as a yield from the land, this still left the question of what it is used for. The short answer is grazing and hay, i.e. animal feed, the end product being meat and dairy products, with the exception of horses, where the end product could be described at the 'entertainment and leisure industry.'

Since the types of crops and associated crop areas are subject to crop rotation and market pressures, the crop distribution in Sparsholt will differ considerably from one year to the next, whereas the change nationwide will be marginal. Arable land takes up around two thirds of all agricultural land. In Sparsholt it is slightly less, with the difference again being accounted for by the absence of sole right rough grazing in the parish.

4.1 Arable crops

The principal activity of landowners in Sparsholt is associated with arable farming. In order to facilitate comparison with what is happening nationwide, I shall use the term 'cultivated land' for what is given in the National Statistics as 'Total tillage and grass including bare fallow land'. Thus, the total area of cultivated land, excluding horse grazing, is around 55% of the total parish area, and compares with 62% nationwide.

So far I have not taken into account what is known as 'set-aside', which is a DEFRA scheme encouraging farmers not to cultivate all their land by giving them subsidies. The idea behind this was twofold: a) to reduce the amount of grain going into the so-called European grain mountain, and b) to promote biodiversity in allowing wildlife to flourish in the uncultivated areas. Nationwide this amounts to just under 5% of cultivated land, and I have no reason to think that it is any different in Sparsholt.

Top of the list of arable crops in the parish in 2008 was

barley, which took up nearly one half of the total cultivated land in the parish, compared with just under 8% nationwide[1]. Of the barley not exported (and exports account for about a quarter of it), 60% goes into animal feed, and the balance into beer and spirits.

Next on the list was grass at 35% of the parish cultivated land. In this figure I have included grass used for horse grazing, although it could be argued that this is not an agricultural activity. This compares with 60% of cultivated land nationwide.

This was followed by oilseed rape at 16% compared with 4.3% nationwide. Oilseed rape is used in cooking and food processing under the general label of vegetable oil. Its recent dramatic rise in production can be attributed to its increasing use as a biofuel suitable for diesel engines, therefore also known as bio-diesel.

Now we come around to wheat. This accounted for just 6% of cultivated land in Sparsholt in 2008, but a whacking 16% nationwide. Well, we all need our daily bread, so it's only right that Britain should jump into the breach and in addition make us self-sufficient on that score anyway. That's what wheat is all about – bread. Isn't it?

The reader, cautioned by my previous rhetorical question pratfalls, will have guessed that it isn't. In fact, 40% of the national wheat crop goes into livestock feed, including incidentally that of our pets. The balance is used in thousands of different food products ranging from cereals, pizzas, flour, sponge puddings and pot noodles to oyster sauce, and, yes, even bread. This, however, requires a higher specification only met by 11% of our current production, with the result that although we export 25% of our total production (some of this even to China), we also import 27%.

Due to the generally lower quality of the wheat produced in the parish, most of it is exported for livestock feed, with the end product eventually finding its way back to our supermarket shelves in the form of imported bacon, continental sausages and other meats. This may also help to explain the considerably lower percentage of wheat grown in the parish, coupled with the fact that there's more money to be made on barley here.

So where does the wheat for our bread come from? Less than half from the EU, the balance from Canada and other countries. And the reason? Bread needs a special grade and quality of wheat which is more difficult to grow here. But it's fine for all the other products, and of course for animal feed. So why do we need to feed all these animals? Because we all (or most of us) eat meat, quite apart from the dairy products which also require animals. Now, with the looming energy crisis, there will be pressure to grow even more for bio-fuel.

The remaining miscellaneous crops grown in the parish and occupying the 4% of agricultural holdings not accounted for so far consist of peas, linseed, maize and opium poppies (see 4.3. below) and also set-aside, which is likely to disappear with the revival of wheat prices, and with the European grain mountain now at bare minimum safety stock level.

For those of us concerned about global warming, or more precisely about the contribution of this attributable to CO_2 emissions, it's worth noting that each meat-eater reportedly accounts for an additional 1.5 tons of CO_2 per annum over and above that produced by vegetarians, and a 2006 report by the United Nations claims that livestock is responsible for 18% of all greenhouse gases[2]. This rather trivialises the emissions attributable to flying, and does make one wonder if the Green Lobby's efforts in this respect would not be better spent persuading us to give up meat. That would certainly result in some spectacular changes in our crop distribution, with fewer crops needed to feed us, since cutting out the meat intermediary would result in a far more efficient energy conversion and corresponding lower CO2 emissions.

4.2 Biofuel Crops

Quite apart from the likelihood of seeing more opium poppies, our crop distribution is set to change again. With the impending oil shortage, oilseed rape for oil for diesel fuel is being grown ever more widely, Our countryside has already taken on a yellow hue for much of the year, with latest statistics showing a massive 20% increase over a couple of years ago. As fossil fuel becomes more expensive due to the reduction in world oil reserves, the use of maize, palm oil, oilseed rape, wheat and sugar beet as raw material for biofuels will become more prevalent. Pilot plants are already operative in Somerset, where the County Council has pioneered its use in subsidising the installation of a processing plant and distribution points for the fuelling of council transport. In addition, a new plant which has come on stream in Kent is likely to stimulate further demand for this product. Another source for bio-fuel will be some of the three to four million tons of surplus wheat we are already exporting to Europe. Any worries about shortage of land for food production can be answered by the fact that we now have some 1.2 million acres of set aside land which, although not suitable for food crops, may well fill the gap for energy.

A word of caution about these speculations; recent calculations carried out by the Co-op Insurance Society show that even a 10% contribution from biofuels for cars alone worldwide would necessitate devoting 9% of all agricultural land to this purpose. This implies that when oil runs out we will have the choice between giving up cars or tightening our belts. Another problem is the further diminution of rainforests which are being cut down to make more land available for profitable bio-fuel. For this reason the current European directive aimed at providing at least 10% of all car fuels from biofuels by 2020 has already given rise to criticisms from the Green Lobby[3].

4.3 Opium

The first time I enquired about a field of white poppies in the parish, I was told they were grown for poppy seed for bread. This information could well be described as poppycock, after further enquiries about the same crop from another source, i.e. the grower, revealed that these poppies were principally grown for their opium content.

Can he be serious, I thought, with visions of informing the Ministry of Defence with a view to getting the nearby Green Jackets Barracks to dispatch a regiment equipped with flamethrowers to put paid to that crop, and earning myself an OBE into the bargain. Well actually, he said, we are licensed to grow opium poppies. They are for Johnson Matthey, who use the crop to make diamorphine for the NHS.

Known worldwide as heroin, its advantage over codeine-based pain-killers is that its lethal dose is a hundred times the effective dose, compared with ten times for codeine. The oriental poppy or *papaver somniferum*, to give it its Latin name, though not significant in terms of total area cultivated in Britain, has a considerable importance to some of us in our lives. The brilliant white tinged with blue poppy flowers first appeared on our landscape as recently as five years ago, and belong to the same family of opium poppies we are currently sending our soldiers out to stop Afghan farmers from growing. This situation appears completely anomalous in light of the fact that the reason for opium being grown in Britain is that there is a shortage of it for processing into diamorphine. This is a less emotive name for heroin, a term coined from the German for 'heroic' by the pharmacologist Heinrich Dreser in 1898, when it was prescribed for the treatment of coughs, chest pains and the discomfort of pneumonia and tuberculosis. In the NHS it is used as a pain-killer for the terminally ill, and in cases of heart attack, injury, surgery and cancers. One of the principal advantages of diamorphine or heroin over morphine is its ease of injection and speed of effectiveness, which is of course also the reason why it is so widely used by drug addicts.

In addition to the morphine extracted from the plant itself, the poppy seeds are used on bread or pressed for cooking oil and even paint base. At present the principal end product of opium grown in this country, however, is diamorphine. The introduction of opium poppy crops to Britain goes back to as recently as 2002, when Macfarlane Smith, the world's largest legal manufacturer of diamorphine, felt it necessary to have some UK suppliers of the raw opium to ensure being able to meet the demand.

This concern has proved to be not only justified but optimistic, since by 2005 a definite shortage of diamorphine was admitted by the Department of Health, which was then cautioning doctors to prescribe morphine instead of diamorphine, the latter to be used mainly in palliative care. This admonition has had an impact upon clinical and patient services in the NHS.[4]

The sudden shortage in supply of the drug appears to be both due to a shortage in the supply of raw poppy straw and processing capability. In any event, the government has authorised an increasing number of farmers to grow opium in Britain, though currently still only around 30 in total. Who these are and where is shrouded in secrecy, and although Sparsholt growers are licensed they have not (so far) been required to sign the Official Secrets Act.

Why there should be this secrecy is a mystery in itself. Perhaps the Government is concerned that illicit drug suppliers might harvest the opium crops in dead of night and do their own processing in urban basements – a rather unlikely situation considering that harvesting is carried out by purpose-built machines provided by the opium processors.

Not surprisingly, leading doctors in the NHS and some European MEPs have suggested buying Afghan opium rather than burning it. Worth noting here is that before it was demonized, in the heyday of the British Empire, we were championing and even enforcing the trade in opium after the Chinese emperor had banned its import. This resulted in the so-called Opium Wars of 1842 and 1856, launched by what has been described as 'the biggest, richest and most aggressive drug cartel the world has ever known' – i.e. the British Empire!

4.4 Timber

Another crop grown in the parish, of a variety not associated with food or drugs, is the timber grown by the Forestry Commission in Sparsholt. In recent years, due to cheap imports from the Baltic countries, the yield from harvesting timber was little more than the cost of harvesting. Due to increasing costs of fuel and thus transportation, imported timber is no longer as cheap as it was. As a result, and coupled with the advent of wood-burning power stations, native timber is in greater demand, heralding a revival in forestry. At the last felling in 2006 West Wood was expected to yield about 20,000 tons of timber to a value of between £2 and £5 per ton paid by the contractors (Forestry Enterprise sub-contracts most of its forestry operations). Future crops are likely to yield considerably more than that.

Nationwide the volume of wood coming from British forests is currently 9 million cubic metres per annum and rising. This represents just about 10% of our national usage of wood products, showing the considerable potential for growth in national income and jobs in this crop sector.

Another factor promising increasing demand for home-grown timber is the growth of environmentally friendly wood-burning power plants such as the Wilton facility in Teeside. The Forestry Commission is already scheduled to supply 20% of the plant's annual wood requirements from its North Yorkshire forests.

Growing timber for energy will not remain solely within the domain of forestry. Under a scheme promoted by DEFRA, farmers are being encouraged to grow 'short-rotation' willow and poplar for power station fuel. 'Short-rotation' in this context means that the crop is harvested, or more appropriately coppiced every three to four years. Together with *miscansus*, a tall, woody grass, and wood fuel from forests, these crops are expected to help achieve a target of 15% of renewable energy by 2015. Under what is known as the Energy Crops Schemes, DEFRA is disbursing up to £1600 per hectare to promote the planting of these so-called bio-mass crops. It looks as though our countryside is set to change again.

4.5 Cattle etc.

The amount of land used for grazing nationwide reflects the demand for meat in our diet. This is considerably less noticeable in Sparsholt, where livestock is a relatively minor end-product compared with cereals, and even then a large proportion of the total grazing in the parish is devoted to horses. The only significant livestock farm in the parish is the one at Sparsholt College, which still devotes some 20% of its activities to agriculture. College land plays a part in the production of both arable crops, livestock and dairy farming in the parish. As already mentioned, pigs, beef and sheep are the principal livestock products, yielding 184 tons of pork, 30 tons of beef and 20 tons of lamb per annum respectively, with the dairy herd contributing an astonishing 1.2 million litres of milk. The deer herd also produces some venison for the market, and no mention has so far been made of the fishing activities. These, over and above providing teaching facilities for students going into fish farming or other related industries, do also have an end product in the form of juvenile salmon supplied to the Environment Agency's River Thames re-stocking programme.

The College livestock includes some 90 horses, ten belonging to the College, which, although not kept for meat, can be regarded as an end-product of sorts. Together with feed crop and grazing areas, they take up about 75% of College arable land. Some of the other farms in the Parish incorporate grazing for beef cattle and sheep, though in the latter case they only 'bring on' sheep for fattening up prior to going for slaughter.

4.6 Horses

The amount of land devoted to horse grazing and stabling in Sparsholt warrants a look at the wider scene. The return on investment is here provided by the whole equestrian establishment, which could be classified as an entertainment and leisure industry. This includes recreational riding, dressage, general riding sport, pony trekking and horseracing. Since foxhunting is now illegal, simulated variations termed 'drag-hunting' and 'trail hunting' are practised instead, until such time, as the hunting fraternity believes, that the Hunting Act making fox-hunting illegal will be repealed. For the moment, there is still a requirement for horses to be kept and trained for drag-hunting, though probably in diminishing numbers.

There is in addition an end product in terms of meat, not one the average horse lover in Britain would want to be associated with, but one which cannot be ignored, bearing in mind that the horse population in the UK is around 1.3 million. With some 35,000 per annum going to abattoirs, the amount of horsemeat produced is not insignificant. One third of it is destined for export to horse-meat consumers in Europe, with the bulk of it going to France. What happens to the other 23,000 horses slaughtered for reasons of injury, terminal illness or chronic conditions annually remains a mystery, promulgated in part by the animal rights campaigners. No abattoir dealing in horsemeat would care to broadcast its activity for fear of becoming a target for some extremist activist.

Few if any horse owners make a living out of bringing on horses for meat, and most would probably be horrified at this being suggested as a possibility. Even the owners of feral ponies roaming the New Forest, Dartmoor and Exmoor, where there is no great personal attachment between man and beast, get their recompense for rearing and caring for what is a significant tourist attraction through selling on to the general recreational riding industry, rather than for meat.

Eventually, however, there remains a need to dispose of ageing and infirm horses and ponies. Until a few years ago some of this was taken care of by the export of live horses for meat to the continent. This export was stopped by an act of parliament which effectively restricted the export of horses to those valued at £5000 and over, which simply meant horses used exclusively for racing or breeding.

In Sparsholt, horse owners are either engaged in keeping horses to ride, or providing livery stabling and/or grazing to other owners, or in bringing on horses for the horse-racing industry. In general, where an owner is not prepared to sell a terminally sick horse on to an abattoir for anything between

£20 and £300, he is eventually faced with the cost of disposing of a horse carcass. This can be considerable, particularly where the owners want to personally witness a humane end for their horse prior to incineration. Horse burial, moreover, though not totally unknown, must be rare. The reasons for this are that few owners have a burial site available, and if they do, probably not the permission required in accordance with regulations pertaining to the fouling of local groundwater sources.

The French claim, with some justification, that since we eat cows and sheep with no reservations, why should we make a distinction for horses, particularly since horsemeat is very palatable. Horse lovers would claim that horses are capable of human emotions and attachments, and have even been described as man's best friend. My own feelings on this are admittedly influenced by my engineering training, which results in my looking at the purely mechanical risks involved in such a small brain being in charge of such a large mass. Whilst quite capable of amiably stroking a muzzle provided it is from the other side of a fence, I am nervous of having not far short of a ton weight of best friend galloping towards me and being affectionately trampled to death.

Historically, since the demise of the mining industry the total number of horses reared in the country has declined from the days when around 70,000 ponies (in 1914) alone were employed in moving coal trucks in mines. These ponies were, according to the heritage centre at Pontypridd, of such vital importance to the operation of the mines that if one were accidentally killed, an instant replacement had to be made, whereas if a miner dropped dead he might not be moved until the next shift!

4.7 What the future holds

The total yield from the land is the end result of an inter-action
of a number of forces. In the case of private landowners, the
principal motivation has to be making a profit from the land,
although for some the attraction of having a home in spacious
grounds far from the madding crowd may well be an additional
consideration. But 'life-style' buyers may soon have to re-think
their priorities. Now that farming has much brighter prospects,
bolstered up by increasing world prices for wheat and barley
resulting from poor harvests attributed to the climatic effects
of global warming, the price of farmland is rocketing by up to
50% compared with a year ago. Additional causes for this are
the extra land required for growing bio-fuel crops, financial
speculation and even continental farmers coming to get a
share of the action. Average annual farm net income has risen
to £38,000 (2007/08 figures)[5], a far cry from the situation in
2004/05 when National Statistics painted a disturbing picture,
with a quarter of all farming enterprises not showing a net
income.

There are a considerable number of constrictions on the
operation of market forces in farming, ranging from Acts of
Parliament resulting from international agreements, such as
the Kyoto Protocol on Biodiversity and the CAP (Common
Agricultural Policy) of the EU, put into effect by DEFRA through
numerous incentives and restrictions. Further pressures
emanate from other bodies already dealt with in Part 1.

Another consideration, that of the national interest in
becoming self-sufficient with regard to our staple food supply,
has been eroded by the advent of the global market, but
still rankles in the minds of some agriculturists. It probably

stems from World War II, when Britain was reliant on convoys bringing in staple foods from across the Atlantic. Everything was rationed, particularly food, and all were encouraged to 'dig for victory', i.e. produce additional food on gardens, allotments, parks or any piece of available green space. In spite of globalisation, this 'siege mentality' persists, and partly accounts for the subsidised agriculture we have become accustomed to.

So our landscape is set to change once again, and unless the Green Lobby can persuade the taxpayer to come up with more subsidies, it will be a case of 'Farewell Biodiversity'. In addition to the yellowing of the landscape due to the spread of Rapeseed, we will also see the spread of miniature forests on farmland. Change is on the way – and fast.

Part 5

Institutions and Charities

Under this heading I have lumped all land occupied and/or run by public bodies or volunteers with a view to providing a service to the community. In the case of the village shop and post office, although its principal purpose is to provide a source of income to the proprietors, I have no doubt whatsoever that it also provides a social forum and meeting point to parishioners, which in my view figures highly in providing a social service.

5.1 The School

In 1850 Sir Frederic H. H. Bathurst, Bart., a local Squire, transferred a parcel of land amounting to half a hectare (1¼ acre), at no cost, to the minister and churchwardens of the parish, for the erection of a school. This gift was, and still is, of considerable benefit to parishioners, although the land now belongs to Hampshire County Council. The original school was designed to accommodate 60 boys, presumably leaving the girls to continue attending the local 'Dame School' located a little further down the road. Dame in this context did not refer to the pupils, but the teacher, and was not meant to signify the type of Dame celebrated in the Broadway musical song 'There's nothing like a Dame', but a lady of impeccable repute and furthermore highly unlikely to infect her pupils with ambitions of going public in any way, least of all in the manner associated with the Hollywood version.

If a reincarnation of Sir Frederic were to visit the result of his beneficence today, he would see a few changes. Instead of pupils sitting in orderly rows of benches listening to the teacher and not speaking unless spoken to by him or her, he would see them sitting around tables in groups and engaging in conversation with the teacher. Sir Frederic might also raise an eyebrow on learning that the cane he was looking for no longer exists. So how do you punish offenders, he might ask. Well if it's really serious, they would be excluded from attending school for a few days. And what misdemeanour would warrant that? The teacher might inadvertently pick on something like – 'Well, little Willie might have told the teacher to 'f... off' – an example he or she would quickly come to regret, as they tried to explain the full meaning of this offence to Sir Frederic without a Victorian dictionary of colloquialisms to hand. By the time the full implication of the offence had sunk in, Sir Frederic might well be muttering something about horsewhipping being too good. If the teacher were then foolish enough to suggest that physical punishment might damage not only little Willie's person and also his self-esteem, he or she might well be responsible for Sir Frederic's resulting heart attack.

Church of England schools make up a quarter of all primary schools in England[1], compared with 10% Roman Catholic and 65% of no religious character. Sparsholt Church of England Voluntary Controlled Primary School, to give it its official name, differs from the Voluntary Aided and Foundation schools in that, although the School is owned by the Church, there is no Church majority on the governing body, and the teachers are employed by the Local Education Authority which also funds repairs and capital projects. It now has 110 pupils, about a quarter drawn from the parish, with the remainder being bussed in or brought by their parents from adjacent parishes.

Stephen Young, the head teacher (illustration 9), is a product of King Alfred's College in Winchester (now Winchester University), and gained his teaching experience both in Winchester and a Test Valley country parish before taking up his post in Sparsholt some seven years ago. He patiently explained (to someone just a little out of touch with current primary school education) the workings of the school. It is of course bound to teach the three core subjects laid down by the National Curriculum, i.e. English, maths, science, followed by IT (Information Technology) and RE (Religious Education), which must not be confused with RI (Religious Instruction), since it deals principally with the historical and relative positions of the various religions.

This elicited some questions from me regarding the extent of the 'Church Controlled' element of the children's education, which, he told me, was confined to having assemblies at the start of every day which contain worship and instruction 'of a broadly Christian character'. At least one of these assemblies each week is taken by the local vicar. Are there any problems with other religious faiths? Not at present, since there are only two pupils from a non-Christian background. In any event, parents are at liberty to request that their children do not have to participate in assemblies, although this has not in fact happened at Sparsholt.

Worth noting here is that in the 2001 census 72% of participants described themselves as Christian. This was followed by a poll taken for BBC News 24's Faith Day in 2005, according to which this figure was only 67%. A more recent Guardian poll in January 2008 puts the figure of believers as low as 37%. This can indicate that either there has been a sudden drastic decline in religiosity, or that those polled were not selected from the same social groups, or that the questions put were not worded identically.

In any event, if these figures are reflected in the parish it would indicate a non-Christian element of between 28% and 63%, large enough to be noted. Since none of the parents have requested that their children do not take part in the daily assembly, one must assume that the non-believer parents are content for their children to participate in some religious observances. As for the Christian element, they have the option of letting their children attend the 'Friday Club', which is a form of Sunday school (i.e. informal Christian religious instruction for children) taken after normal school hours by the vicar on Friday afternoons. Currently the number of children staying on for this varies from 10 to 15.

Broadly on the subject of behavioural education, Stephen Young elaborated on a new acronym I had to learn, which was PSHE (Personal, Social and Health Education), defined as 'comprising all aspects of schools' planned provision to promote their children's personal, social development including health and well-being". A further subject allied to PSHE is Citizenship, which includes, amongst other items, imparting 'the knowledge, skills and values relevant to the nature and practices of participative democracy – .....and the value to individuals... of involvement in the local and wider community – ...and an awareness of world affairs – ...

and the economic realities of adult life'. Phew! The whole of the above is of course a pretty wide-ranging subject, and for more mature readers the curriculum will seem a far cry from the three Rs they were brought up with, particularly since we have not as yet touched on other subjects taught in addition to the core subjects, such as History, Geography, Art and Design and Music, all in the form of 'integrated subjects' (i.e. not taught as a subject in their own right but integrated with the other curriculum subjects), and then there is still PE (Physical Education). The latter is facilitated by the adjacent village hall (see below) which in addition provides the venue for the daily assemblies and lunch. Outside there is a sports field, which is leased from the Martineau Will Trust on a six yearly renewable basis, and also incorporates a small pond and nature reserve created by the school.

The school is maintained by the Hampshire Education Authority and is run by a board of governors, four of whom are appointed by the parents, two by the local Education Authority, two by the Foundation (the vicar and another diocesan appointee), two are staff, one is a Parish Council representative and one is co-opted.

The ethnic make-up of the pupils is currently principally white, with just two non-white children, i.e. less than 2% This compares with a figure of 8% nationwide, and with densities of non-white pupils exceeding whites in some London boroughs. Yet of all the 'maintained' schools, less than 1% are non-Christian. Current trends indicate that this relatively low percentage is bound to rise.

Local pride prompts me to add that Sparsholt Primary School is rated well above average in performance by Ofsted, who considered it 'a good school with a number of outstanding aspects' particularly in regard to the pupils' personal development. In spite of this, quite a few parishioners choose to send their children to private schools outside the parish.

On the wider scene, a recent Unicef (United Nations Childrens' Fund) report puts the UK at the bottom of a list of 21 economically advanced countries as far as the 'wellbeing of children and adolescents' is concerned, though in this respect also Sparsholt appears to be well above average in the UK.

Access to the surrounding countryside is good, with a footpath running alongside the school. On closer inspection, however, it becomes apparent that any walks undertaken by school groups to the local country park entail a considerable detour in order to avoid using the direct route along the main road through the village which has no footway, quite apart from being narrow and hazardous due to traffic most of the time. This means that even just getting to the local Ham Green Common entails a return walk of one and a half miles for the children.

5.2 The Church

The Church no longer owns any land in the parish, apart from St Stephen's Church and the graveyard. The most recent land transactions of significance involving the Church were in 1993 and 2000, when it disposed of its remaining land in the parish. Figures for the situation in England are virtually impossible to come by, since the Diocesan boards of finance who account for some 90% of the Church's real estate are either unwilling or unable to supply this information, but a recent guesstimate is that the Church still rates around fourteenth in the Landowner stakes, with approximately 60,000 ha (135,000 acres). This shows a drastic decline from the days of the last prior records in 'The return of the Owners of Land' of 1872, when the grand total of the land owned or controlled by the Church was estimated at 860,000ha (2,130,000 acres).

To find out more about the Church's drastic decline of land tenure in the parish of Sparsholt in recent years, i.e. from several hundred hectares to nothing (apart from the Church itself and the adjoining graveyard), I approached 'the Dean and Chapter' of Winchester for information. This led, after a desultory correspondence, to the Church Commissioners and thence to the Archivist at the Church of England Record Centre, who informed me that they had historical records relating to my quest which could be made available to me for viewing at the Lambeth Palace Library.

This turned out to be an unrewarding pilgrimage, though it did get me an entrée to this august establishment. The entrance to it is a romantically placed small gate in the Palace wall with a piece of paper pinned to it requesting visitors to the Library to ring the bell, which is activated by an ancient bell yoke. This I did, and after what seemed a long silence, I heard footsteps approaching. After a further interval and unlocking noises, the door swung open revealing a young woman who proceeded to guide me through a garden and courtyard, followed by a series of corridors, to the inner sanctum. This consisted of a large room with wall-to-wall bookshelves crammed to the ceiling with religious reference works, and several elderly ladies perusing these at long tables accompanied by a deafening silence.

I quietly joined them to inspect the files waiting for me, only to discover that these dealt only with a prolonged correspondence between an incumbent at St Stephen's in Sparsholt and the Bishop about his request to extend the vicarage vegetable garden.

I was now at the end of my tether, and decided that a detailed account of the decline of Church landownership in the parish will have to wait the arrival of a younger researcher with time to spare (around 50 years, I should think). There is a recent figure for Hampshire, where the Church still owns 1,170 ha (2,900 acres).[1]

Although St Stephen's Church has been at the centre of village life for many centuries, in an increasingly secular society its importance in the community has declined. Together with the graveyard it belongs to the Diocese of Winchester and is administered by the Parochial Church Council, who look after the necessary maintenance work on the building and graveyard.

In keeping with my original brief of finding out what people who occupy land in the parish do which is of social significance, I approached the vicar, the Revd. Juliet Montague (illustration 10), to get some idea of how she sees her 'Mission' in Sparsholt. As it happened, she had only recently seen her domain extend to incorporate another two parishes, and is now in charge of what has been renamed the 'Downs Benefice' consisting of five parishes and their churches.

So how much of her time has she left to devote to Sparsholt? This, she told me, is variable. In addition to any services and visits to parishioners, during term time she has regular school visits for taking assembly at least once in the week, plus the weekly 'Friday School', which is an hour tacked on after normal school hours, and effectively substitutes for what was commonly known as Sunday School. Now designed to incorporate a more populist emphasis, she described it as an opportunity for children to have fun with Christian activities based on story, song, prayer and craft.

She gave me an example of what this entails by telling me what her last Friday School was about. It concerned the story of the paralysed man, and the children were shown, with the aid of models they made up with the assistance of Juliet and a voluntary helper, how a paralysed person has to be cared for.

Of course I immediately cottoned on to what this was leading up to, and jumped in with the surmise that this was really an extension of a lesson in citizenship, that is to say showing the children how to care for the disabled. The vicar kindly ignored my gaffe and went on to say that this was to illustrate the story of Jesus curing the paralysed man. A subsequent intensive bible study by me revealed that this episode was also the origin of Jesus's immortal phrase 'take up thy bed and walk'.

An example of topics raised by her during assembly would be to bring across the Christian abhorrence of bullying of any kind, and needless to say school playground bullying in particular. And how did she see her mission in Sparsholt in general? To build relationships with parishioners, to spread the message that the Church is there to help everybody, and particularly of course those who are looking for help, like the elderly and infirm. The emphasis on the various aspects of her stewardship varies from one parish to another, and is established by her in conjunction with the Parochial Church Council for each parish.

This is not to say that she doesn't believe in having fun, and the Church wants people to engage in social functions organised by the Church or in conjunction with it wherever possible, be it coffee mornings, village fetes or the annual thanksgiving dinner at the village hall.

Peter May, one of the regular worshippers and also churchwarden and member of the Parochial Church Council for some 50 years, put current church attendance on Sundays as being about 25 parishioners plus another 5 from outside the parish. In response to my questions he also informed me about the money side of the Church, in particular the stipend of the vicar, which to one not familiar with ecclesiastical matters came as somewhat of a surprise.

I had always assumed that the vicar is an employee of 'the Church', and that his (or her, in this case) salary would come out of the Church's coffers, end of story. The question of where this money came from was simply answered, in my mind anyway, by: the Church must have a lot of income from rents of its still considerable landholdings, and wealthy benefactors in addition, to meet its running costs.

Over recent years there had been tales of unwise investments on the part of the Church Commissioners leaving the Church with significant losses to make up, and the already mentioned sale of the remaining Church lands in Sparsholt should have prepared me for what I now learnt. This was that the Diocese (Winchester, in this case), does pay the vicar, and the running costs of the Diocese, and then simply bills the PCC (Parochial Church Council) for its share of this. It is then the PCCs responsibility to come up with the money, which it does, by means of covenants from beneficent parishioners, usually as a notional percentage of their income, say 1% for argument, coupled with collections taken at services.

Special refurbishments such as, in recent years, the bells and the organ, were financed through the generosity of individual parishioners and special fund-raising events organised by members of the congregation. An example of the latter was the recent 'Hymnathon', when a well known local organist provided a 24hour organ recital which helped to raise £35,000 for the organ restoration, some of this, I can't help conjecturing, needed by the extra wear and tear imposed on it by the event.

Any refurbishments necessary to deal with routine maintenance is in addition met, in part, by a local charity, the 'Friends of St Stephen's' which jumps into the breach, or even breaches, as they might occur, by raising funds toward the maintenance of the fabric of the Church.

The remaining land owned by the Church and undoubtedly fulfilling a social function is the graveyard, which extends to some 0.3 ha (¾ acres), with the larger part now occupied by the graves of villagers going back to the 12th century, and harbouring the remains of some 4000 parishioners.

The cost of reserving a plot in the cemetery is now £110, which goes to the Diocese, plus an extra £80 which goes to the parish. Four plots are currently already reserved, presumably by parishioners who are particular about their final resting place, possibly regarding the situation (desirable residence, deceptively small, with extensive views of the Church ?). There is no rental payable, so we must assume that the plots are freehold. But are they registered with the Land Registry? And how long can the tenants remain there with the pressure on land being what it is? Of the 4000 residents only 400 are remembered with a visible gravestone, and the oldest legible one I found was dated 1830.

A further aspect of the Church's social activities, and one we are all familiar with, whether we like it or not (some actually don't), is the ringing of the bells. Bell-ringing is an art that has to be taught, and bell-ringers are therefore of necessity a dedicated lot. They give up their time on a regular basis to call the faithful to prayer on Sundays, and at various other occasions such as weddings and funerals. Collectively they are known as 'bands', and their skill not only consists in knowing when to let the rope slip through their hands to avoid being hoisted up into the belfry. If that were all that was to it, we would all be regularly assaulted by a cacophony of clashing bells, which, with mostly six bells on the go, might well suffice to waken the dead in addition to those who had spent too long at the pub the previous night.

Even being woken by harmonious bell-ringing at 9 o'clock on a Sunday morning has brought forth some adverse comment from those living near to the Church. Little do they realise what sufferings their more urban counterparts are subjected to in parishes where the church clock not only strikes the hours, but the quarter hours as well, and all that for 24 hours a day. More mature readers might remember the film *Genevieve* about the adventures of two couples competing in the annual London to Brighton vintage car race who, after a strenuous day on the road finally collapsed into bed in the early hours, only to be roused almost immediately by the crashing of the bells from the church tower opposite.

I note that in our more urban society this is giving rise

9　Stephen Young, Head Teacher: no caning

10　Juliette Montague, the vicar, and Peter May, church warden:
pillars of the church

11   Linda Scorey (right) and Stella Neaves outside Alladin's cave

12   Norris and Pam Fuller and National Trust Cottages: deserving
villagers

to anger and litigation, particularly where the relevant authorities have not relaxed the 24-hour ringing. A recent case was brought by Mid Beds District Council in the way of a noise abatement order on behalf of bell-shocked residents who claimed to be suffering from sleepless nights. It was thrown out by the Bedford Magistrates Court on the basis that they considered that the bells were a quintessential part of English village life, and the Council was fined £7400 to boot. The magistrates failed to offer any advice to the insomniac residents. Earplugs might possibly do the trick, but are they quintessentially English village life?

It's good to know that our European partners are also having bell-ringing problems. During a recent visit to Munich I read about a similar action being taken by a suburban community there. They succeeded in restricting the ringing to between 8am and 10 pm – a good compromise, I thought, though when it comes to Sparsholt, 9am on a Sunday is just about acceptable.

Timing is of the essence in bell-ringing, and having witnessed a ringing session I was struck by the concentration required throughout the ringing, which normally lasts around 20 minutes. The practice of 'ringing the changes', meaning a succession of notes in various sequences, is uniquely English. A further extension of this is the ringing of a peal, which means ringing every possible sequence of the bells. If there are eight bells, the number of changes is 5040, and this usually takes about three and a half hours. All this, I have been assured, is quite easy to work out, particularly if you are a Cambridge graduate with a mathematics degree. My informant was, as it happened, and I am still waiting to pass all this on to the next person that tells me they have just heard a peal of bells.

I also discovered in my researches that continental bells (other than the multiple carillon type) are often bigger, and swing only over a relatively small arc, whereas the English Bells are mounted to permit one full revolution, to permit them to come to rest upside down. Getting these bells to move at all, considering that they might weigh up to several tons, would appear to be an impossible task to a rank outsider like myself. The answer is a simple mechanical device called the headstock, the yoke-like frame supporting the bells which also incorporates the pivotal bearings, permitting these to be placed nearer the centre of gravity of the bells, thereby reducing the prevalence of hernias amongst bell-ringers.

One of the village old-timers, John Cleverly, the 'tower captain', as he should be designated, of the 'band' and a bell-ringer of many years standing (and ringing), has the daunting task of ensuring that there is a full complement of ringers available at all times, or at least a minimum of four, in addition to arranging for bell-practice and initiation of new ringers. When not engaged in waking up the residents, he also attends to the maintenance of the churchyard, whose inhabitants are beyond being disturbed even by the mightiest clashing of bells.

5.3 The Village Hall

There are a little under 8900 village halls spread around England. Their importance in village life is varied, and depends on their distance from the nearest major conurbation offering alternative facilities. Traditionally the main users are local voluntary organisations such as playgroups, parent and toddler groups, senior citizens' clubs, youth clubs and Women's Institutes. This mix differs somewhat in Sparsholt, partly due to its proximity to the centre of Winchester just three miles away, and partly due to its close association with the village school.

The original Sparsholt village hall, known as the Memorial Hall, was a timber building erected after the First World War on land given to the parish by Samuel Bostock, onetime owner of Lainston Manor and thereafter of Sparsholt manor. It was replaced by the existing brick Memorial Hall in 1982, and is run by a dedicated group of volunteers, including (and I have to declare an interest here) Marie Bush, my spouse and current secretary, not necessarily or always in that order.

Her task is a demanding one, and I should know since I spend some of my (for her information, valuable) time answering telephone calls to pass on messages usually concerning some problems which have arisen at 'the Hall'. Just as a taster of examples (and cautionary ones at that for those thinking of taking up equivalent office elsewhere) these might range from the Women's Institute meetings complaining about the heat having gone off, or the caretaker finding the floor has come up or the ceiling down, or the Brownies' summer camp being faced with starvation because the cooker has exploded or constipation because the drains are blocked, or when can the plumber expect to be paid. I could write a book about all that alone – and I'm only the messenger!

As a sweetener to keep her at it, the Trustees also asked her to chair the Entertainments Committee, a position which has its rewards in allowing her to have a spot on BBC Solent advertising the latest offerings at the Hall, which have ranged from a condensed dramatised version of 'Aesop's Fables' to an evening of Latin American music.

The Memorial Hall fills a special place in the local community because of its close association with the village primary school, which leases most of the building during normal school hours. This is of course advantageous to the trustees, i.e. the village hall committee, since it simplifies the on-going problem of keeping it occupied in order to raise the necessary funds for hall running costs, currently around £15,000 per annum. This does, however, curtail its availability for other daytime functions during term times, an obvious case of not being able to have it both ways.

For the remaining time the hall provides the usual amenities of a village hall, such as a venue for the monthly parish council meetings, Women's Institute meetings, fitness and yoga sessions, weddings and other family celebrations, plus occasional lettings for the Local History Society, badminton and short tennis clubs, the National Photographic Society, the aforementioned Brownies etc. Then there are the entertainments organised by local charities such as the Friends of St Stephen's, the annual Harvest Supper organised by the Church, and other annual events celebrating national anniversaries such as Burns night.

In addition to these, the entertainment committee of the Memorial Hall organises a number of performances put on by a variety of theatrical and other groups and individuals, mostly accompanied by a cooked meal served in the interval by a group of dedicated committee members and others, mostly, I have to concede, ladies, with a noticeable minority of one or two gentlemen. And all these give their time and sweat in the interests of bringing parishioners together and thus providing more social cohesion. This has resulted in some memorable evenings over the past few years when all were able to let their hair down, and even get out there and wiggle their bottoms to the music. The committee has also organised special day-time sessions for the children, one event being a training session for aspiring young jugglers and tightrope walkers.

The aforementioned secretary and spouse is passionate about stimulating social life in the village. Her activity could, I suppose, be regarded as an extension of the vicar's mission from promoting a dialogue with God to promoting a dialogue amongst the villagers. They have both come up against the difficulty of luring people away from their home shrine, a situation exacerbated by the fact that many local families are sustained by husbands, even sometimes wives, who have to commute some distance to work or are away from home for at least a part of the week.

5.4 The Shop and Post Office

The shop and post office are incorporated in the Well House Store, a square brick building occupying 0.003 ha. It is just 12 ½ ft square inside, and allowing for shop and post office counters, has space for not more than six customers standing in close proximity. This actually allows, or even necessitates, the rubbing of elbows amongst the clientele, a form of social contact which should, in my view, be encouraged. Where and when else do all classes of the village mingle in such good-humoured groups motivated by the same common purpose:

to purchase some of the huge stock of goodies and/or services provided by this little Aladdin's Cave, and dispensed with such quiet and efficient expertise by the two lady proprietors.

Linda Scorey and Stella Neaves (illustration 11) acquired the lease of the building from the Parish Council in 1994, and pioneered its use as a general store and post office. They had known each other from the days some 30 years ago when they were both County Commissioners for the Girl Guides. In the interim Linda had worked part-time for a Housing Association, and Stella as an almoner at a local hospital, but they decided it was time to try their hands at something new.

Although the building had been used by an assortment of other businesses including a picture framer and a dealer in imported artefacts, its use as a general store required considerable additional storage space. This was provided by a rather unusual extension of the building – not adding to it, but converting the 6000 gallon tank originally used for storing the parish's water supply and occupying the whole of the upper storey of the building, into a store room, an innovative and perhaps unique conversion pioneered by David Stockwell, the then Chairman of the Parish Council.

At this juncture I should explain that the origin of the tank is closely connected with the name of the business, i.e. the Well House, since the building was originally constructed over a well in 1897, financed by a rate on the parish. An engine-powered pump eventually replaced a short-lived brave attempt at using a wind turbine to raise the water from some 250ft below the ground into the tank, from where it was distributed to the parishioners. In 1908 the well became redundant when Samuel Bostock, the local squire at the time, organised a pipeline supply to the village from a reservoir at Crab Wood near the parish boundary.

The current use of the original tank as storage space would no doubt attract an accolade from environmental campaigners, even though they might have felt cheated by the abandonment of the wind turbine. It was accomplished by making an opening in the bottom of the tank large enough to provide a stairwell access into the tank, which now also accommodates a WC – surely minimalist thinking on a grand scale!

Although water no longer flows from the well, the range of goods and services flowing into the village from the Well House Stores is impressive: – everything from a torch battery and phone card through fresh fruit and vegetables, local farm eggs, canned goods of all descriptions, newspapers, post cards and greeting cards, sweets of all kinds and of course the usual post office services including a facility for providing foreign currency at a day's notice. Even freshly baked bread, supplied by Lainston House Hotel's own bakery just up the road is available to the villagers.

The shop does not offer loans, apart from short-term like the ones I manage to swing when I find I've left my money at home. There is also a generous display board for local entrepreneurs to offer their services, which range from computer help through gardening and general handwork to keep fit classes and yoga (no home massage on offer, as far as I could see after close scrutiny).

A gold mine? Well certainly to the villagers, and unfortunately also to the criminal fraternity, whose first fully frontal onslaught in the dead of night resulted in the removal of the front door followed by that of the safe. Surprising, then, that no one has attempted to load the whole building on to a truck and make off with it. This was followed by other incidents over the years, including two hold-ups, one of which resulted in Linda being injured. Linda and Stella's joint resolution, however, was to carry on regardless, and this courage has earned them the gratitude of the village expressed by a plaque from the Parish Council, together with a commendation by the Chief Constable of the Hampshire Police Force.

The recent closure by the government of some 3000 rural post offices sent a nervous tremor through the village. Although Sparsholt got a reprieve, there were angry demonstrations in the adjacent Parish when it became known that its post office was on the black list. Pensioners and Yuppies joined forces and bombarded our MP with letters and e-mails. No eggs were thrown and no one was hurt, apart from feelings of course. Just another example of what happens when market forces and the public are at loggerheads.

5.5 The Pubs

When it comes to social significance, the pubs must surely take pride of place. Most inhabitants of this sceptred isle will have been in one at least once in their lives, and quite a lot will have spent as much of their waking lives there as they have at home. Whether this is a national trend or not, the latter group is not prominent at Sparsholt, though I have to rely on hearsay on this matter since my own annual attendances can usually be counted on the fingers of two hands.

One aspect I can pronounce on with some certainty without reference to the horse's mouth is this: our local pub scene has changed an awful lot since my first forays into The Plough in the days when dining out was more of a week-end activity, unless associated with special treats on birthdays or other anniversaries and special occasions. The dining area was laid out in military precision in two rows of tables, monitored at the far end by the landlord behind the bar, who, in addition to taking orders, kept a stern eye on the proceedings. In accordance with the gravity of the occasion, conversation was in subdued tones accentuated by the occasional scraping of knives on plates, and a watchful eye and ear was kept on what the Joneses were doing there and why.

Credit cards were not known on the local scene, nor was tipping to any significant degree. On the harder drinking (rather than eating) side, there were certainly more local lads propping up the public bar or indulging in bar billiards and darts, something that has gone, at least from The Plough. The Rack and Manger on the outer fringe of Sparsholt is another story, principally because it caters to a greater degree for Sparsholt College students and locals who are more into a social drink than a meal.

The current scene at The Plough is one of customers enjoying food and drink in that order, in the convivial atmosphere generated by good cooking and a mix of customers, mostly from outside the village, partaking in a relaxed and often quite noisy atmosphere, certainly loud enough to drown out any scraping of knives on plates. The young staff consisting of around a dozen full-timers backed up by more than thirty part-timers (in total, that is, and I have this on authority from the landlord, Richard Crawford, the publican for over thirteen years), help to promote a cheerful and informal scene, reinforced by a small retinue of drinkers at the bar. One particularly noticeable aspect of change is the increasing number of parents accompanied by their children amongst the clientele, sometimes even quite late in the day, which indicates that we are beginning to take a leaf out of our continental neighbours' books.

The drinking/driving bans have without doubt brought about a significant change in the role of country pubs, and particularly those whose clientele do not live within walking distance. In order to continue making a living from customers who are no longer able to safely consume more than a modest amount of alcohol, the only course open to the publicans was to become purveyors of food, which they did in ever greater numbers. Inevitably, pool tables and dartboards had to make room for tables and chairs, and so had some of the likely lads who used to frequent the public bars.

The owner of The Plough is Wadsworth Brewery, who also own the adjacent field, which provides grazing for a couple of donkeys and thus an additional attraction for visitors' children, and brings the brewery's landholding in the parish up to a grand total of just under 1ha. In terms of the total number of people partaking of the services it provides, this land could be argued to harbour the single most important social institution in the village next to the village hall, in addition to providing employment to some villagers, although the bulk of the staff come from further afield. Of the local employees, most are teenagers between 14 and 18 years old, and spend between one and three four-hour shifts a week helping with the washing up and preparation of food. Although this is not necessarily the principal aim of the pubs in employing youngsters, it cannot be denied that they help them to acquire lifetime skills as far as giving them a feeling of the importance of managing money when they realise it has to be worked for.

The other local pub, the Rack and Manger, is located at the Parish boundary away from the centre of the village, but closer and more accessible to Sparsholt College. It is therefore patronised more by staff and students of the college, who can be sure of meals at affordable prices, particularly since the new tenant has experience of feeding hungry multitudes, having also been the catering manager at Winchester Prison. He also provides local employment for youngsters in the bar.

6. The National Trust and others

Few locals are aware that there is a National Trust property in the village, because it is neither signposted nor open to the public. The Vaine cottages must be one of the smallest landholdings of the National Trust, which owns 223,000 ha (550,000 acres) in England and Wales, making it one of the largest landowners in the UK next to the Forestry Commission and the Ministry of Defence.

The cottages were originally given to the parish by one Sir George Buckston Browne, whose wife Elizabeth (nee Vaine) had once lived there, to be occupied by parishioners who deserved well of the parish. These are currently Pam and Norris Fuller (illustration 12), occupying one half, and Irene Minns the other half. Norris Fuller was, during his working life, the manager of Church Farm belonging to the Martineau family, and as such has been of invaluable assistance to me regarding farming matters, not only how to tell wheat from chaff, but also from barley! His wife Pam has been a leading member of the local WI for as long as she has lived in the village, let's just say since the late fifties. Irene Minns, the widow of the onetime chairman of the village hall, has been associated with it ever since it was built, latterly as caretaker.

Of the remaining institutions and charities in the parish, the principal one associated with land is the cricket club. Sparsholt Cricket Club is the owner of the 'Norman Edward field,' named after one of its founder members, a one time parishioner. It extends to 1 ha (2.5 acres), and was given to the club by Samuel Bostock, that indefatigable local benefactor, in the 1930s, bringing the total land area donated by him to local institutions to 1.3 ha (3.2 acres). The brick pavilion at the far end of the field was erected largely by craftsmen club members in 1982 . Am I reading something of social significance into this by expressing surprise that a cricket club should have so many craftsmen members, or were they just committed DIY'ers?

However this should be, the club has gone from strength to strength, and now boasts several elevens. I should hasten to say that I am really not qualified to judge the full significance of this, having been struck on the head by a cricket ball at the tender age of thirteen when I was supposed to be fielding and my attention had wavered, as it has done increasingly over subsequent years where ball games are concerned, possibly more so due to the injury sustained at the time.

A further social comment I am bound to make is about the rise and demise of the local football club, set up on a field leased to it by another local landowner for the purpose. There was also a pavilion erected by craftsmen members, albeit not of brick, and its abandoned remains are still there to act as a reminder that there is not the same drive behind this sport in our village. Perhaps a part of the problem was the rather steep slope of the filed, which must have imposed extra exertions on the players just keeping up with the ball rolling downhill. Alas, even that is no longer possible now, since a multitude of molehills would put a stop to any rolling balls.

An institution of equal, perhaps of even greater, national import, although it occupies land in the village only intermittently by means of regular meetings in the village hall, is the WI. Several of its local members have been such for times, dare I say it, immemorial? If not, certainly memorable. The current WI is no longer 'all jam and Jerusalem', a denigrating phrase used mainly by chauvinist pigs and implying an overriding interest in jam making and the singing of the rousing hymn '*Jerusalem*' set to Blake's poem ending with '*till we have built Jerusalem in England's green and pleasant land*' to inaugurate their meetings. This ritual is no longer obligatory, perhaps because Blake's lofty sentiment might now be frowned on by those who abhor any building on our green land!

WI meetings mostly have a speaker on various topics of interest to women, with a historical emphasis on activities connected with the home, and (lucky chauvinists) the kitchen, including, even, home preserves. Moving with the times, however, they now also encompass history, recycling and exploring the local environment. Women's Lib protagonists might argue it would be a good thing if men engaged in similar activities devoted to learning more about home, car and garden maintenance, thus reducing the time they have to spend in front of the telly watching ball games and consuming gallons of inebriating substances.

A recent film under the title 'Calendar Girls' and featuring some of Britain's best known actresses, portrayed the WI in a new and slightly shocking light, with members being photographed without their clothes on, though partly hidden by strategically placed decorous items. The moral of the film was that if it's in a good cause and you can't beat them (i.e. the tabloids), join them!

Closely related in earnest endeavour, and no doubt replicated in almost equal numbers across the nation, is the Local History Society, of which I proudly proclaim myself a member. We also occasionally occupy the village hall, though not as frequently as the WI. Under the leadership of our Secretary, Elizabeth May, and often entertained by her acerbic wit, the society has illuminated various aspects of both local and even far flung history. I refer in particular to an address by Edgar Feuchtwanger, a Sparsholt resident for over 40 years, nephew of the world renowned author of *Jew Süss* and himself an eminent historian. He told us about his youth in Nazi Germany, where he lived in Munich just a hundred yards down the road from Hitler's flat, and witnessed some of Hitler's comings and goings there between 1929 and 1936. He ruefully commented that he is better known because of this association than for his numerous biographies of German and English Statesmen, and, latterly, his biography *Albert and Victoria*.

More recently the society hosted a talk by the author of a biography of Evelyn Dunbar, the painter whose picture of a wartime land girl now hangs in the Tate Gallery (see Part 6/1 – 'Heritage found').

A local charity not widely known, and occupying still less land, in fact no more than a room in the author's abode, is the Gwen Bush Foundation, set up in memory of my first wife in order to fund research into alleviation of pain. It got into the public eye in 2001 when it was nominated a Mayor of Winchester charity and hosted, amongst other events, an interview conducted by Debbie Thrower, our patron, with Esther Rantzen, Peter White and Matt le Tissier.

Part 6

Our heritage

When it comes to defining who owns what, I have taken 'the land' as constituting 'what'. I have looked at what the owners are doing with it which is of social significance. What I have not done so far is to look at what the owners inherited with the land they occupy, i.e. the heritage that came with it. By this I am referring to 'anything that has been transmitted from the past or handed down by tradition'.

The natural environment of earth, heath, woods, hills, mountains, rivers, sea and sky, together with what we have imprinted on it with our own puny efforts by making use of what nature put at our disposal, is all 'our' heritage, regardless of whether we own it or not. Just digging up the land to grow crops was enough to change the face of our environment beyond recognition from the time we started doing so around 10,000 BC, and in this and other ways we are continuing to add to our heritage for future generations.

Metaphorically digging up what I consider to be significant items of heritage in my own parish brought home to me the idea that since we are all interconnected through culture and upbringing, whatever I find in Sparsholt will be of significance to the wider community. Furthermore, it might stimulate those readers who are also townies living in the countryside, or just interested in what goes on there, to do some investigating in their own areas.

1. Heritage found

If we want to know what our forebears did or thought, we usually go to a museum. What we find there might well have been dug up from somewhere practically next door to where we live. Other clues to what life was like before us are contained in the landscape and the remains of ancient buildings on it, but putting these clues together requires an intimate knowledge of local history beyond most of us.

Future generations will have no trouble finding out what we did, or thought. It's all on the worldwide web. Their problem will not be the scarcity of information, but its overwhelming abundance. We will be well-documented, even though 'we' are now a multitude undreamt of by our forbears. Once we were content with finding out about the thoughts and deeds of the rich and the powerful – the kings and queens, the nobles and bishops, the admirals and the generals, even artists and writers who had achieved fame in their lifetime. We scoured our churches for the inscriptions on their memorial stones and sarcophagi, their epitaphs and lifetime CVs brimming with heroic deeds on and off the battlefields. They were the few that mattered.

All that's changed. Now we all matter, even if not to the same degree. Everyone, we are told, will be famous for fifteen minutes, at least. There are even plans to let those who feel so inclined to stand on a plinth in Trafalgar Square for an hour. One wonders whether the originals of the adjacent statues there might be turning in their graves.

There would in any event not be room for commemorative gravestones for everyone, but the chances are that some aspects of our lives will be recorded on a computer hard-drive somewhere. Associating us with a building or a piece of land will be much more difficult, however, since in our mobile society we seldom stay in one place for any length of time. On the positive side, although there will be a lot more of us to be remembered, there will also be a lot more who will think us worth remembering.

Heritage is generally taken to mean old relics or ruins of buildings which go back hundreds, sometimes thousands of years. Added to these are the remains and artefacts of previous generations, ranging from Victorian anchovy jars and Roman pottery and jewellery to iron age tools, all still discovered after years of metal detector activities. Skulls and bones are unearthed by building works or just land-slides caused by heavy rain. Museums might well be bursting at the seams, but for those with neither the time nor the inclination to visit them a few explanatory tablets on site might go a long way to awakening local interest in what went before. Yet even the site of the Sparsholt Roman villa is not marked in any way.

This is all the more puzzling when even the Parish Council could afford to have a large signboard placed in the centre of the village adjacent to the main through-road but facing away from it into the village hall car park, with a beautifully executed map of the village showing the locations of major points of interest together with all the public footpaths in the parish. Unfortunately, the information on the board could not be described as being informative, since the main points of interest shown, such as the church and the post office, are practically adjacent to it. As for the odd rambler who might have used it to locate the local pub, this is the one item on the map shown incorrectly located along the wrong lane, and in a field. Who knows how many ramblers or even just walkers have perished of dehydration and/or exhaustion in this corner of a field, searching for The Plough Inn.

The point of all this is that there is public money available to provide both superfluous and also misleading information, yet the site of the Roman villa has nothing to commemorate it for the benefit of what is probably a considerable number of interested parties.

In Sparsholt, as indeed most villages in England, the most significant item of heritage must be the Church. St Stephen's, which dates back to Saxon times, stands on a knoll reputedly once a pagan holy site. In keeping with pagan traditions, the original foundations were built over animal or human sacrificial remains, the latter sometimes the remains of a malefactor. This was partly corroborated during repairs carried out in 1883, when it was found that one corner of the church's foundations rested on an open grave, the contents of which were unfortunately not examined, but disposed of by the workmen. Whether the remains were those of a malefactor has therefore not been established.

Apart from a chalk coffin originally found in a grave under the reading desk complete with occupant (both in fair condition), which has now been placed outside the church (but without the occupant), St Stephen's is well equipped with the usual relics of local worthies, with plaques commemorating their lives, noteworthy perhaps for their relative dearth of military achievements.

The remains of another ecclesiastical building, St Peter's Chapel (illustration 14) alongside Lainston House, contain large engraved gravestones of some of the residents of Lainston House, including those of relatives of the notorious Elizabeth Chudleigh, the courtier and eventually Duchess of Kingston, whose first marriage took place here. If heritage can be said to include an association with historical personages, Elizabeth Chudleigh would certainly rank highly in Sparsholt heritage. I do not know of any other resident who has been the subject of several biographies, or, more to the point, whose life has been accompanied by such notoriety. From the time she appeared at one of George II's balls in a provocatively diaphanous gown, to her trial in the House of Lords for bigamy, she entertained and shocked society in equal measure by her brazen disregard of conventional morality. Having been found guilty of bigamy, but not branded in the palm since she could claim exemption on the grounds of being an aristocrat, she was hounded out of the country by the disinherited descendants of her second husband, the Duke of Kingston. Although she returned to England only briefly in later years, she was able to use this inheritance to finance a lifestyle abroad which encompassed buying an estate in St Petersburg and entertaining Catherine the Great at lavish parties there.

Lainston House, where Elizabeth Chudleigh had lived for a while under the tutelage of her aunt, is now the hotel. It goes back to the 18th century, though remains of the original foundations located in the cellar are claimed to go back to the 11th or 12th century. The existing building was erected on the remains of an Elizabethan house, parts of which are still visible in the form of mullioned windows in a part of the basement. Charles II is reputed to have stayed there with his mistress at the time when he was considering incorporating the House within a grand park stretching Northwest from his palace in Winchester.

Lainston House Hotel, which it has now become, has provided comforts for an ex-prime minister and an ex-president, and I am referring to Margaret Thatcher and ex-president George (without the W) Bush. Both have stayed there on several occasions, she to work on her biography, and he to polish his fly-fishing technique. To my knowledge, there was no hanky-panky involved, and on the only occasion they were staying there together, this was due to coincidence rather then a planned rendezvous. What a let-down after Elizabeth Chudleigh, who would turn in her grave in Paris if she knew. Another heritage feature associated with Lainston House is the adjacent 18th century dovecote which reputedly housed up to eight hundred doves, but is no longer occupied.

A notable building from more recent times is the Well House in the village, constructed in 1897 over the original well, with a steam engine to power a pump which was used to top up the tank under the roof twice a week. The engine proved unreliable, and was later supplemented by a windmill alongside the brick building. This water supply became obsolete after water was piped to the village from a reservoir situated near Crab Wood, and the Well House ceased to be used for its original purpose in 1916. Since those days it has served a variety of enterprises, currently the Well House Stores as already mentioned. Some of the remaining listed buildings scattered around the parish mainly go back to the 16th and 17th centuries.

Another house of more recent origin and now known as Chapel Cottage, since it originally was a Methodist Chapel, has a special significance to me, since I knew its first occupant, one Miss Cynthia Stocker. Since she died many years ago, she will forgive me for referring to her as heritage, but that is what she was to me. She came from that stoic breed of upper class women who formed the backbone of the British Empire. Known to have been a senior administrator in the Red Cross in Italy at the end of the war, she was already in her mid eighties when I became a neighbour on the opposite side of the road. Our initial efforts to get to know her were rebuffed when she told us she didn't go to parties. She did however invite us over 'for sherry', which in my case was amended to a tumbler of rum since she understood this was more of a man's drink. This assumption took me by surprise, and I can only assume it came from the naval connection in her family, probably dating back to Nelson.

My lack of naval experience, coupled with total ignorance of the inebriating effects of this potion, unfortunately dimmed my recollections of the event. However, in spite of my subsequent alcoholic haze I recall her telling us about her disciplinarian father bringing his two daughters up the 'right way' by teaching them how to carry out routine maintenance on the family's Morris Cowley car. This entailed Cynthia, (reputedly named after her father's favourite bloodhound) being in charge of the regular replacement of spark plugs while her sister stood by with a fire extinguisher, ready for all contingencies.

Not surprising then that Miss Stocker, even in old age was no laggard when it came to 'motors'. I remember in particular one winter's day when traffic in and out of the village was brought to a halt by six inches of snow. There was a deathly hush as the snowflakes drifted down. Curtains were twitching as everyone waited for someone else to make the first move.

13   St. Peter's chapel: scandalous heritage

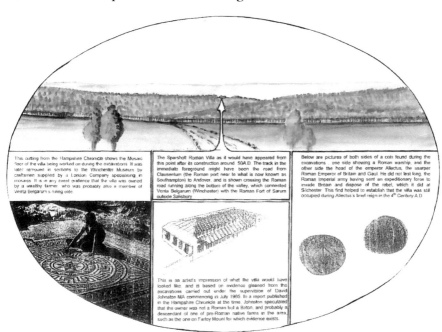

14   Roman villa signboard proposal: all my own work

15a Village old-timer Ted Salter: 'They're not hollows, they're bomb
craters'

15b Unnatural hollows? Tracy Mathews, Winchester Heritage Officer,
in bit of a hole

It was Miss Stocker who did. Her Mini sprang into life with a splutter and a roar, and off she careered down the lane into Winchester leaving a snaking pattern in the snow for less stalwart souls to follow what for her was obviously not a difficult act.

Another piece of local heritage are the Vaine Cottages already mentioned above under 'National Trust'. Their donation to the village by Sir George Buckston Browne was occasioned by the fact that his wife, borne Elizabeth Vaine, grew up there. She was later sponsored by the vicar to enable her to train as a nurse in London, where she met Buckston Browne. As a result Sparsholt now has a tenuous connection with Charles Darwin. This happened because Buckston Browne was evidently a great admirer of Darwin, and personally put up the money for the purchase of Darwin's residence, Down House in Kent, to be used as a museum to Darwin. It could therefore be said that in addition to buying the Vaine Cottages for Sparsholt in memory of his wife, Buckston Browne bought Down House for the nation to commemorate Charles Darwin.

Apart from heritage artefacts in the Church, it is worth noting that a well known painting associated with Sparsholt College and dating back to the last war now hangs in the Tate Gallery. At that time Sparsholt College was used as a training establishment for 'Land Girls', more accurately members of the Women's Land Army. Some of the recruits in training were painted by Evelyn Dunbar, the only woman to be appointed an official war artist by the Government in 1940. She is now acknowledged as one of Britain's most notable war artists. One of her best known paintings of land girls, painted at Sparsholt at that time and entitled 'A Land Girl and the Bail

Bull' now hangs in the Tate Gallery (see illustration 15a). She also contributed sketches to a training manual for new recruits (illustration 15b), and has recently become the subject of a new a biography by Dr Gill Clarke, who gave a talk on this to the Sparsholt History Society shortly after publication of her book in 2008.

Readily available and tangible pieces of heritage can be found amongst the flints in the ploughed fields of the parish, and more valuable items defined as treasure trove. This, according to the current Treasure Act, may consist of any metallic objects at least 300 years old, provided that no less than 10% by weight of the metal is precious metal (i.e. gold or silver), or any item more than 200 years old and deemed by the Secretary of State to be of outstanding historical, archaeological or cultural importance. And once again, we are reminded that all such finds ultimately belong to the Crown. Well, bully for the Crown, you might say, but if I find anything I'm going to hang on to it. If you do, however, you'd be breaking the law.

In order to encourage treasure hunters not to break the law and keep supplying our museums with interesting historical artefacts, the Government introduced 'The Portable Antiquities Scheme' in 1997. This entitles the finder and landowner together to a reward equivalent to the market price for the find, as established by a panel of experts appointed by the Government. If no public museum is willing or able to purchase at this price, the item reverts to the ownership of the finder and landowner to keep or sell on the open market.

Currently about 90% of all finds are reported by metal detector enthusiasts, and the number of finds each year has gone up by 20% and more each year. A record find in 2001 in a parish not many miles away, consisting of an iron age gold necklace together with other decorative items, now referred to collectively as the Winchester Hoard, was valued at £350,000. It was purchased for the British Museum in London, where it is now on display.

This has prompted me to look carefully at any items thrown up after local ploughing, and I am now the proud owner of a fossilised sea urchin between 65 and 95 million years old. Or so I was told by the Hampshire Museum Service after submitting it to their scrutiny. Whilst they politely described my find as interesting, I did come away with the distinct impression that fossilised sea urchins are as common as muck, and certainly there was no hint of the museum expressing a fervent desire to acquire it. Looks as though I will have to get myself a metal detector to get anywhere.

On the subject of heritage the question of what is happening on the land is of obvious importance. Quite apart from any development activities resulting in a diminution of the qualities we deem important in our environment, there is the increasing problem of rubbish pollution by users of the countryside, in addition to the illegal tipping of building materials or household waste such as refrigerators and furniture at any convenient (to the rubbisher) location. The CPRE (Campaign for the Protection of Rural England) under its new president, Bill Bryson, the American author known for his assessment of Britain in his book 'Notes from a Small Island', has done some acerbic research on the sheer volume of rubbish deposited in our countryside in a year. It currently stands at 25 million tonnes, and rising.

Coming, as Bill Bryson does, from the flatlands of Iowa where people who walk across the land for pleasure are likely to be detained by the local sheriff prior to being released into the custody of a psychiatric institution, one can sympathise with his anger at seeing our lovely countryside rubbished by a relatively small number of environmental thugs. Public flogging for those caught in the act springs to mind, particularly in view of evidence that this or similar harsh punishment has worked miracles in clearing the streets of Singapore of chewing gum. Whilst the CPRE does not go as far as proposing this as a solution in England, it is in favour of heavily fining litter louts and fly-tippers caught in the act. More importantly, it wants people to put pressure on local authorities to do more to apprehend these vandals, in addition to removing the accumulating rubbish promptly.

Just in case we think this rubbish is all due to 'townies' and weekend walkers, it is worth noting that DEFRA recently put the figure for the amount of plastics used by the farming industry at 86,000 tonnes per annum, and I for one have seen some of this being blown around our fields – so even farmers are no laggards when it comes to the 'just drop it – nobody will notice' syndrome.

2. Heritage lost

A specific site of local heritage interest which is lost to the parish is the site of the Roman villa which was excavated in West Wood in 1965. The villa's mosaic floor was removed reasonably intact with the aid of an expert from Italy and transferred to Winchester City museum together with other finds. Not many years ago I proposed the erection of a signboard (see illustration 13) to commemorate the villa and the excavations, supported by Sparsholt History Society and David Johnston, who was the man in charge of the original excavations. The idea was for the signboard to be erected at the car park overlooking the site and just over half a mile from it, with the suggestion to place an additional plaque at the actual site, where no traces of the villa or the excavations remain.

My hope that this effort would fire up the relevant people at Hampshire County Council was, however, unfounded. Or perhaps it did, and the resulting temporary excitement led to subsequent exhaustion followed by permanent inactivity. In fairness, I was informed at the time that the matter was being looked at again, but that there had been objections to similar proposals in the past on the basis that: a) signboards are invariably vandalised, and b), the marking of the site would make it a focal point for travellers and/or all-night unofficial rock concerts.

These objections could of course be levelled against the marking of any historical sites. Since the Roman villa was of significance great enough to warrant the excavation of the mosaic floor, just placing an explanatory plaque on the site, or at least in the car park overlooking it, appears to be a reasonable proposition. David Johnston had, in the meantime, been instrumental in the erection of a mosaic signboard on a public space overlooking the site of another Roman villa at nearby Kingsworthy. The problem in getting a similar signboard erected at West Wood appeared to be caused by the inability of each of the major players, i.e. English Heritage, Hampshire County Council and the Forestry Commission, to agree on who was going to shoulder the cost involved.

When it comes to archaeological heritage sites, there are several in the parish worth mentioning, such as the two large tumuli in West Wood. In common with the Roman villa site the absence of any signboards explaining their significance is a regrettable lapse on the part of the County Recreation and Heritage department.

For those with an inquisitive mind, clues to what went on hundreds of years ago abound. It's not just trees which by their size alone show how long they've been around, but so-called medieval wood banks signifying the boundary of a property. Heritage can encompass a great variety of things, including even just holes in the ground, such as the hollows resembling craters to be found in Crab Wood. When I first noticed them, they reminded me of an experience some years ago in a Dorset wood when I came across a German student measuring up a similar hollow. He told me that this was a unique geological feature known as 'Natural Hollows' to be found in that part of the world. Furthermore, he was writing a thesis on them.

This experience prompted me to jump to the conclusion that the Crab Wood hollows were just further samples of these geological features, only to be enlightened by Ted Salter (illustration 16a), a village old-timer, who laughed knowingly at this explanation. 'They're not natural,' he said, 'they're bomb craters. I knew the village constable who lived here during the war, and he wrote it up in a book.' So where would I be able to see this book? Well, it was never printed. It was just in handwriting. He's been dead for years, but his daughter can probably lay her hands on it. And where does she live? Don't know, but my sister might.

16a   Land Army Girls at Sparsholt: Elizabeth Dunbar Painting

READY TO MILK

16b   and Instruction manual excerpt

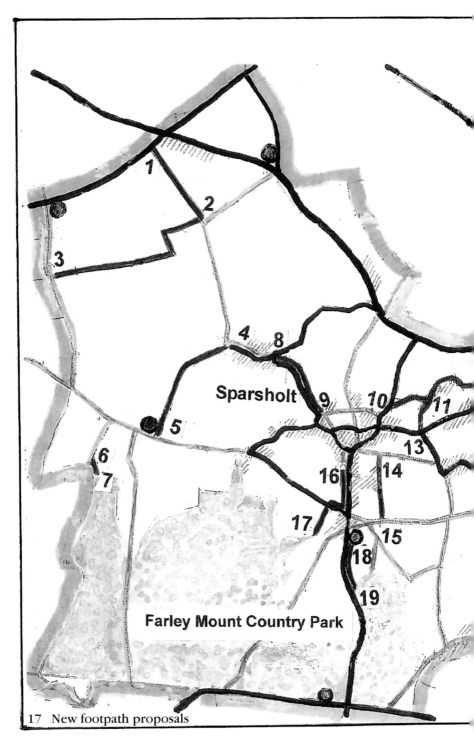

Sparsholt

Farley Mount Country Park

17   New footpath proposals

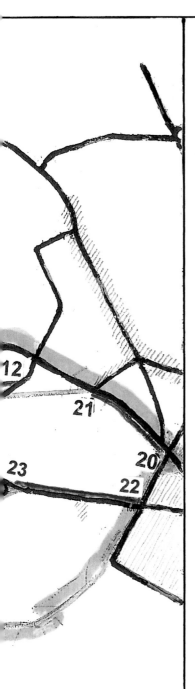

Sparsholt Rights of Way Map
Right of way (ROW) defined as:
footpath, bridle-way or byway

Existing ROW and car park

Proposed ROW and car park

Public Road

Parish Boundary

Woodland

Housing

New ROW Junction Numbers **16**

Proposed New Links

Ref No	Purpose
1-2	village to Stockbridge
2-3	village circular
4-5	village circular
6-7	village circular
8-9	village circular
10-11-12	circular from Winchester
12-11-13	circular from Winchester
14-15	village to common
16-17	village to West Wood
18-19	Ham Green to Crab Wood
20-21	circular from Winchester
22-23	circular from Winchester

Well, his sister knew someone who might tell me where I could find the person who knew the daughter of the special constable who wrote about the bombs. But in the meantime, she said, her husband knew about the hollows, and he says they are dew ponds. He used to live near there as a boy and paddle in them. And he says there weren't any bombs dropped there anyway.

Then I met someone who knew someone who lived in the village during the war, and she knew what they were. They were craters from unexploded bombs brought there from Southampton during the war and detonated.

However, whilst searching for evidence at the local reference library regarding this story and the whole question of bombs dropped in the area during the war, I bumped into a fellow member of the Sparsholt History Society. In the course of exchanging pleasantries I told him about my quest at the library. He smiled knowingly and informed me he had been taken around Crab Wood with the WI by a Forestry Guide, who had explained that the hollows were medieval pig pens. Could he tell me how to locate this guide? No, but he was from the Forestry and had ginger hair.

This was where the matter rested, until curiosity got the better of me and I went prospecting for these natural hollows, dew ponds or bomb craters. Turns out there are at the very least sixteen of them, and counting. But my researches at the Hampshire Records office revealed that only one or two bombs were dropped in Sparsholt, and certainly not over sixteen together on Crab Wood.

So I tackled Jo Baker, the Senior Ranger at Crab Wood depot to see if she could help me locate the ginger-haired originator of the medieval pig pens story. Well, he's been retired for a couple of years. In any case, she has made a map of the hollows some while ago, and she believes they are Dene holes. Dene holes? Yes – basically chalk mines with vertical access shafts no bigger than a metre in diameter going down to excavations as far as 20 to 30 metres below ground level, where they mined the chalk which was reputed to be particularly beneficial as a top dressing for arable land. In any case, she remembers hearing that Southampton University did a trial dig in the 70s, so why don't I ask them about it. I did, but they had no records pertaining to this.

In a final act of desperation I contacted the Hampshire County Archaeology department, who eventually referred me to Tracy Matthews (illustration 16b), the Winchester District Historic Heritage officer. She consented to being photographed inside a hollow, but her interest waned when no obvious and convincing information was forthcoming from the Hampshire Archives.

So who is right? Or perhaps they all are? Perhaps there are one or several of each? I have to confess that the idea of the stick of bombs jettisoned by a German Bomber on the way home had its attractions. I could see myself going on a jolly to the Luftwaffe Headquarters to research and track down a Fritz, or Hans, or maybe Wolfgang who might have released the bombs, though the chances that they would still be alive (or myself, for that matter, by the time I had tracked them down) appeared a bit slim.

Another piece of local heritage in danger of becoming lost are the remains of what were major droves through the parish. One of them, referred to in the book on Sparsholt by Cecilia

Knowles[1] as 'the Ox Drove', and now in part existing as a paved country lane, is not even commemorated as such either in the way of a road sign or on local maps. Yet at one time, not even two centuries ago, it was probably used by Welsh drovers to get their cattle to Portsmouth, as witnessed by the existence of the 'Drovers House' in Stockbridge just a few miles to the west. It carries an inscription in Welsh (now partly obliterated by later alterations to the building) which, so we are told, broadly means 'Hay seasoned, pasture delicious, beer good and bed comfortable.' And who could ask for more?

Cecilia Knowles also refers to a 'Bull Drove' going up the hill from the Ox Drove, past an inn called the King Billy, and an adjacent windmill, all now gone without a trace. Further conjecture about the use of nearby 'No mans land', another piece of forgotten heritage, as a watering and resting place for the drovers' cattle is reinforced by the existence of a bridleway shown leading to it from the adjacent parish of Ashley, and named 'The Drove' on the 1870 Ordnance Survey maps.

Few records exist about the lives of the drovers, even though they were probably more skilled and adventurous than the cowboys of the American Wild West. Drove roads have been in existence since the domestication of cattle in neolithic times, and reached their heyday around the 18th century. By the late 16th century cattle were being driven from Wales, Scotland and Ireland as far as Kent and the Home Counties. The droves were usually marked by yews in Hampshire, and the Droving Inns were called 'Hutts'.

Although drovers were known to be respected members of the farming community, they must have been of an adventurous disposition. They were away from their homes for weeks and even months at a time, driving herds of cattle and sheep to markets often hundreds of miles away, and carrying documents and money from the sales. If the brief description of them by Robert Louis Stephenson in his book *St Ives* is anything to go by, they could be a bit on the shady side as well. Yet they are not celebrated in print or film like their fellow cowboys in the Wild West, perhaps because they didn't get involved in gunfights with Indians and cattle rustlers. Yet they had to be prepared to defend themselves against thieves, both of money and cattle, and were armed with everything from cudgels and knives to pistols.

Perhaps the reason for the Welsh drovers not making good fictional heroes was that they tended to avoid confrontational situations. It's one thing to have Billy the Kid from Wyoming reaching for his six shooter whilst squinting at his opponent from under his Stetson, and quite another for William Evans bach from Rhosllanerchrugog doing the same from under his felt hat. Just taking the time necessary to identify himself would have given his opponent an unfair advantage.

For another thing, Welsh drovers were unlikely to have spent their nights under a blanket out in the open as their American counterparts did, since they would probably have died of hypothermia or drowning. More likely they were instrumental in the setting up of our world-renowned B & B's.

Part 7

Access

Britain now has approximately 24 million landowners[1]. Of these, the great majority own just a little more than the ground their dwelling stands on. Agricultural land accounts for about 70% of the total land area of England[2]. and were it not for the public rights of way which have been fought for and defended over many years by organisations such as the Ramblers' Association and the Open Spaces Society, we would be unable to walk across any of this.

Even then we are channelled by hedgerows, walls, fences and barbed wire along certain routes established over centuries of usage and/or horse-trading which are now referred to as 'definitive rights of way'. Beyond these, and even after the enactment of the 'Freedom to Roam' legislation (the CROW Act) we cannot walk through woods, fields or along coasts and riverbanks unless these are within a national park, Forestry Commission land or on areas defined as mountain, moor, heath or down.

The reason for this is that the landowners, or their agents, consider any movement across their land away from these definitive rights of way as undesirable if not harmful to their interests. The justifications for this attitude are disputed by those of us who want more access, and who consider that it is the extent to which we are willing to share this with others both from inside and outside our communities which should inform our thinking about access in the countryside.

Back in 1932, an event occurred in the Peak District outside Manchester which had far-reaching consequences for access to the countryside. It was known as the Kinder Scout Trespass, when some 500 walkers went on an organised trespass on to what was mountain and moor in protest against the refusal of the Duke of Devonshire to open a footpath across land which was used solely on a couple of weeks in the year for grouse shooting. This has to be seen in the context that only around 1% of the Peak District land had any kind of public access. Several of the trespassers were later arrested and some were jailed for several months. The ramifications of this event led to wider access to the countryside, and eventually to the 'Freedom to Roam' Act. Although this sounds as though the battle is as good as won, a closer scrutiny reveals that this is far from so.

7.1 Where we can't walk

Access to the countryside has been a particular concern of mine for many years. By upbringing and background a city dweller, the countryside had been a target for me and my family at weekends and annual holidays for as far back as I can remember. This has not changed even though in later years I have been lucky in being able to live in close proximity to it. Exploring it on foot has invariably given me great satisfaction, both from an exercise and an aesthetic point of view. The vistas open to us all in terms of combinations of landscape, seasons, weather, cloudscape, time of day, light and shade are almost infinite, and with such a palette to delight the eye who needs art galleries!

It therefore never fails to surprise me that not all can appreciate this, and more so that the landowners who are the final arbiters of where we can walk invariably see us as intruders. Certainly the private landowners I spoke to on the subject were unanimous in not wanting further access over and above existing rights of way, and furthermore, not at any price. Even the public landowners had some reservations on access, as I shall explain anon.

The reasons for this antipathy on the part of the private landowners are obvious to them, but not to the rest of us. Historically it is the urbanisation of society which is partly responsible. In times when most of the population lived and worked 'on' the land rather than alongside it, what we now fondly, though in my view misguidedly, refer to as the freedom to roam was universally accepted. Most traffic was on foot, and walking to school, church, pub or even your nearest neighbour would entail treks of at least one if not several miles. In those circumstances 'the beaten track' would have been more or less the shortest distance between these centres of communal activities, and were used as what we now refer to as public rights of way.

In law all land had a legal owner, and where there was no claimant, it was deemed to belong to the Monarch. Often the Lords of the Manor had no wish to farm all their land themselves, and let it to those willing and able to do so. This resulted in a multiplicity of tenancies where the notion of trespass would have led to enormous complications, and access to the land was on the basis of 'common' usage regulated by Manorial Courts[3]. Trespass as such was not a punishable offence, though poachers could face a prison sentence or even transportation to the Australian penal colonies for poaching associated with violence.[3]

The eventual enclosure of most of the land was spearheaded by the larger landholders in the interests of agricultural efficiency, and led to the break-up of the Manorial Courts, accompanied by an increasing awareness of who owned what and a formal definition of trespass. This increasing awareness of what was theirs and theirs alone, combined with a rapidly growing urban population straining at the seams to get out on to the land for recreation and a breath of fresh air, resulted in the landowners relapsing into a siege mentality which has persisted since the industrial revolution. The people wanting to cross their land were no longer tenant farmers or farm labourers and their families, or villagers, but strangers from the cities. They trampled on crops, left field gates open, let their dogs run free on land reserved for game and shooting, and even set up tents to camp in.

The landowners decided that their land needed to be protected from this invasion, and that is just what they did, largely aided by the invention of barbed wire in America in 1874 by one Joseph Glidden, who became one of its richest men. This is not surprising considering that barbed wire helped to open up the great American West by making it easier for settlers to fence their land. In Britain it didn't so much open up the West as fence in the livestock and keep out trespassers, not necessarily in that order. Even in this day and age, just one British barbed wire manufacturer claims his product could stretch five times around the world, failing to mention that the bulk of it goes into the home market.

Barbed wire also has a worldwide historical association with restraining humanity in one form or another, ranging from the World War I trenches to World War II concentration camps, not to mention inestimable miles of international frontiers. Appropriately, the human rights campaigning organisation Amnesty International has adopted a graphic representation of it in its logo as a symbol of human oppression.

Not long ago I came across a version of the product finished in a silvery blue metallic paint, perhaps an attempt to make it more attractive, if not just more durable. I, for one, find it difficult to appreciate its aesthetic qualities. Even though its use is gradually diminishing with the advent of the electric fence, there is still a lot of it about. My own contacts with it, limited though painful, have left an indelible impression on me, fortunately not of a physical nature. It goes back to an occasion when my spouse and I were traversing a field in another parish not a million miles away, and on a public footpath, let me say right away! The field was also occupied by a cow and a bull. The latter, after fixing us with an unremitting stare, proceeded in our direction not exactly at a trot but certainly in a purposeful manner, with head down. We promptly broke the law by leaving the designated footpath and headed for the barbed wire fence, with the bull, head still down, by this time trotting after us. A scramble over the fence left us bloodstained, with torn clothing and shaken, and the bull visibly disappointed.

This is just one example where access to the land, though safe in theory, is angled against the public. Safe in theory because, we were later informed, the landowner whose bull we found threatening was in his rights since the bull was of a specific non-offensive breed (it obviously fooled us) and accompanied by a cow. Again in theory, this latter feature is obviously intended to keep the bull's attention focussed on his own affairs, but even a bull can occasionally let his interest wander, particularly if given an opportunity to frighten some ramblers witless. In any event, it would have taken a braver man than me to rely on theory in this case, and had I done so (and survived) I would have been accused of being sexist by standing my ground. A no-win situation, if ever there was one.

Finding a sign at the far end of the footpath in question with the message 'Beware Bull in Field' did little to reassure us that the farmer in question had our safety in mind, rather than wanting to deter the public from using a public footpath. It could be argued that if he felt there was some risk involved to users of the path, it should have been his responsibility to remove the risk instead of putting up a sign about it. Indeed, a fellow rambler has pointed out that had we been attacked by the bull (and could produce evidence to that effect), the farmer would have been liable to prosecution. In the event, by avoiding the risk of being gored, I would have been unable to produce this evidence.

It all reminded me of what in retrospect I feel was a more honest sign I once came across in Ireland which read 'If you think you can cross this field in a couple of minutes, don't try it – our bull can do it in 20 seconds flat'.

Examples of landowner hostility are numerous in my experience, even though never of a violent nature, but mostly irritating and sometimes offensive. One occasion immediately springs to mind, again in another parish, where we were taking a stroll with our Sunday lunch picnic at the ready. We eventually settled under some trees adjacent to a wooden fence near to the path we had come on. We were enjoying the picnic whilst gazing out over the adjacent paddocks containing horses, with a large house in the distance, and a group of people standing in front of it. After a little while this group broke up, and three members of it commenced to move in our direction.

At this stage we didn't take much notice, thinking that they were approaching to inspect one of the horses. Eventually it became clear, however, that we were in fact their destination, and their spokesperson eventually addressed us in an accent which left little doubt as to his social affiliations, enquiring whether we were aware that we were trespassing. We pointed out that we were just 10 metres away from the footpath, to which he responded that footpaths were there to be followed but not deviated from.

It might have been better if he and his minions had then used 'reasonable force' to move us back on to the footpath. Instead, he added to our chagrin by stating that we could finish our sandwiches where we sat as long as we left immediately we had swallowed the last morsel. He failed to add, but this was implied, that if it ever happened again, we might have to face deportation to the colonies.

Just where the law stands on this matter is not quite clear. It states that on a public footpath 'the public has a right to pass and re-pass and for purposes reasonably incidental thereto', and allows for stopping to look at the view, talk to a passer by (big deal, that!), take a photograph and have a picnic on the verge. It does not define 'the verge,' nor, if walking in a group this would entail walking in single file in order to obviate the possibility of blocking the way to walkers in the opposite direction. Presumably if a rambler stops on a footpath for any reason, he is interfering with the rights of others to pass and re-pass. But perhaps I am getting too pedantic in my eagerness to lampoon unnecessary restrictions imposed on walkers

The legal aspects of trespass have always mystified me. The law states, for example, that the landowner may use 'reasonable force' to expel the trespasser from his land. But how can the trespasser, particularly if he is not aware that he is trespassing, be certain that the challenger is in fact the landowner, or even his agent? Nowhere have I seen any requirement for the challenger to produce reasonable credentials as to his authority before using reasonable force. For all I know, he may be a trespasser himself, or just a practical joker, or even a poacher. The law, as is often the case, appears to be 'a ass' in this one as well.

Another frequent event spoiling access to the countryside for walkers is the closure and/or re-location of footpaths. One case in an adjoining parish springs to mind, concerning a path I had walked for some years with my family alongside a wood on top of a hill overlooking the adjacent valley and enjoying extensive distant views. One day we came across a notice at the start of the path stating it had been re-directed around the other side of the wood. This new route, it quickly became evident, was far less attractive. In any event, the old route was the one still shown on my Ordnance Survey map, so I felt justified in re-tracing our steps to it. As often happens to me on these occasions, the owner (presumably, because he acted as though he was) was there to meet us where the old route finally re-joined the new one. He pointed out that we were trespassing, to which I replied by saying that I had walked the old route for some years, and asked why it had it been diverted. The answer was brief and to the point: 'I bring my family for picnics along there.'

This brings me neatly to the old adage which some of my non-walking (or non-trespassing) friends often come up with. 'How would you like it', they say, usually with a satisfied smirk lingering, 'if someone trespassed on your garden?' By now, I have my answer ready: 'My garden is only a small fraction of a hectare. If it were a hundred, I wouldn't feel entitled to mind.'

Another characteristic of landownership in Britain is the secrecy surrounding the owners. Here is an anecdote to illustrate this. We were walking in Hampshire (for security reasons relating to the Data Protection Act I cannot be more specific than that!), and down what was then known as a RUPP (road used as a public footpath), now re-classified as an RB (restricted byway), alongside a high brick wall shielding a mansion some distance away from the public gaze. As we approached the archway incorporating the entrance to the property, a man wearing something like a chauffeur's uniform stepped out of the shrubbery and looked at us with a stony expression. We looked back. 'Good morning', we said, 'nice day'. No response. 'And who might live in this magnificent house?' Stony face relented and regaled us with the statement 'I am not at liberty to divulge that information.'

Our curiosity now thoroughly aroused but unrequited, we moved on. It seemed the only sensible thing to do, particularly since failing to do so might have made us guilty of loitering with intent. Intent to what, you might ask. Intent on finding out who lived in the big house, of course.

Some time after the incident, we perchance met someone who actually lived close by the scene of our encounter. 'That's Andrew Lloyd-Webber's place', he told us. 'He applied to have the public right of way diverted because he feels vulnerable to prying eyes. But us locals objected and won the day.'

Another feature of walking in the countryside on footpaths running close to dwellings has become more prominent in recent years. I am referring to having to cross the immaculate lawns of these dwellings, after negotiating stiles at each end. In many cases the original gardens appear to have been extended to incorporate the footpath, sometimes, I suspect, with the purpose in mind of eventually claiming adverse possession. This is a legal possibility where land is 'squatted' on for a minimum of 12 years without challenge by the previous owner, with 'Private Property' signs in place. So what's my problem with this, as long as I can still walk there? Simply that I am usually charged by some wildly barking overfed mastiff which then proceeds not to savage me, but bury its slobbering schnozzle in my crutch, whilst its owner continues mowing his lawn studiously ignoring me.

The whole question of 'adverse possession' of footpaths which could be the subject of a historical claim of usage by the public is one that needs further investigation. In one instance, which happened in our parish, the owner succeeded both in his claim for adverse possession and closure of what was regarded by some parishioners and even the Winchester Ramblers' Association as a public right of way.

Further afield, landowner applications for footpath diversions often hit the local, and sometimes even the national press headlines, particularly where the owners simply block the path and argue about it later, as was the case with the footpath through the Sussex estate of one Nicholas van Hoogstraten, a landowner well known to ramblers for having referred to them as 'the great unwashed'. Without knowing, or perhaps caring, where, how or even if van Hoogstraten gathered the information to back up this statement, it is undoubtedly aimed at offending ramblers. Presumably his ire against them was aroused because the Ramblers' Association did not gracefully allow him to divert a public right of way because it suited him, but stuck out for their rights and succeeded. Without wishing to imply that van Hoogstraten's action was typical for landowners in general in terms of its virulence, my own experience does indicate that there is an underlying attitude problem of landowners with regard to public access.

The access situation in Sparsholt itself is, according to our major landowners, adequately served by footpaths. 'If you haven't got enough in the parish, you've got the whole of the rest of Hampshire open to you,' I have been told. But why should we have to stray further when our own parish has so many just as attractive local walks available that do not require us to go anywhere by car? Is it another aspect of the mobile society that the further we are from our home ground, the more attractive and interesting the countryside gets? What makes the landowners' paranoia about having the general public on their land all the more ludicrous is the consideration that it's the same public's taxes that are pumping never ending subsidies into their land.

So let's have a look at what we've got available in the way of public rights of way in our parish. Here, I may claim to speak with some authority, having once 'walked' the Sparsholt parish footpaths on behalf of the Winchester branch of the Ramblers' Association. The parish has 9.5 miles in total of footpaths (which in this context includes bridleways, RBs (Restricted Byways) and BOATs (Byways Open to All Traffic, but mostly restricted to non-motorised traffic). With a total land area of the parish of 5.8 square miles, this works out at 1.7 miles of footpath per square mile, the average for England being 2.2 miles. Is there any reason why this should not be enough?

Well, yes, since there is no good reason why it should. Most people who walk would want to do a circular walk in the sense of not wanting to retrace their steps for at least most of the route. And although 9.5 miles sounds a reasonable length, much of this distance would apply only to persons traversing the parish to another destination, and not to locals just wanting to do a circular walk. In addition, many of the longer paths end at a busy main road, and one is a cul-de-sac, both features which I assume are associated with the 1952 drive to get parishes to list which rights of way they wanted to be put on the definitive map, without making sure that they co-ordinated these with adjoining parishes.

Before looking at the provision for circular walks in the parish, certain pre-conditions need to be established. The first and obvious one would have to be that no part of the route will run along a busy main road, unless this has a footway, and even then not more than for one tenth of a mile at most. Another condition would be that not more than one quarter of a mile should be along any lane without a footway that carries traffic in excess of 30 vehicles per hour at any time, since this would be unpleasant at best and hazardous at worst, particularly for walkers accompanied by children or dogs.

Based on these pre-conditions, there is not a single circular walk possible from and incorporating the centre of the village. The reader might well be surprised, when checking for circular walks in his own parish, how prevalent this situation is countrywide. Although by driving to the nearest official car parks in Farley Mount Country Park it would be possible to take three or four circular walks of a hour's duration from there, this still leaves more than half the parish without any circular routes.

All this might also come as a surprise to Sparsholt Parish Council, who published a booklet entitled 'Sparsholt Walks and Rides' in 1996, aided and abetted by Hampshire County Council and the Countryside Commission. This booklet describes six circular walks in the parish. None of these meet the preconditions mentioned above, and one of them has since been closed after a lengthy wrangle associated with adverse possession of the land crossed by the footpath. One wonders how many of the councillors ever attempted any of these walks.

However, the provision of a single link consisting of a footway along part of the route marked 16-17 on the parish map (illustration 17) would bring three of the remaining five walks into compliance with the above preconditions. My map shows the existing rights of way in green, and includes proposals for new links, shown in red, which would increase the number of circular walks available to villagers by around ten, effectively adding another four miles of footpaths. In so doing, the proposals would, in addition, provide Winchester city dwellers with footpath access to Sparsholt village from the city boundary, and long distance walkers with alternative links to the Clarendon Way, the only long-distance route in the parish.

Readers might well consider these proposals revolutionary, and not far short of an incitement to a mass-trespass. Closer inspection, however, will reveal that they mostly constitute no more than field edge paths which would cause minimal interference with farming activities. Indeed, two such paths have been negotiated by DEFRA on a permissive basis (i.e. ten year renewable) just outside the parish boundary already.

For visitors from outside the parish, the provision of additional car parking is essential in any attempt to open up the countryside to walkers from adjacent conurbations. Although in Sparsholt village itself there is a car park which is owned by the Village Hall, it is not a public car park. It has an agreement granting parking to the school staff in addition to people renting the hall for functions. By special arrangement it is also used by people attending the church, but that still does not make it a public car park, and this has provoked some controversy in the community. The Village Hall secretary often finds herself in the unenviable position of having to warn off unofficial parkers at times when the car park is temporarily empty.

For readers who think I am labouring the point, I should explain that being frequently engaged on walking excursions throughout the county, I have become aware of similar problems encountered in other parishes. A quick inspection of local maps will confirm that few if any villages have official car parks designated as such. There is only one in the parish of Sparsholt, and that is right on its boundary and about as far as one can get from the village centre.

Village centre car parking might well be provided by local pubs, or exist simply in the form of on-street parking. The former is subject to the obvious pressure to patronize the pub, the latter involves creating a nuisance and, in narrow country lanes, a possible hazard to other road users. All this implies that nationwide the provision of village centre car parks should meet with more consideration if we are serious about getting people to walk.

A significant aspect of the closer look at rights of way in the parish showed that there are virtually none over more than half of the parish area, except for a few that end on a main road on the parish boundary. This prompted me to mark in links in red, mainly along field borders and including routes with exceptional views which would improve this situation dramatically. Finally, throwing all caution to the wind, I gave my imagination full reign and marked in the additional car parking along public roads that would facilitate circular walks with red blobs.

To readers who might be interested in doing the same on their own parish maps, but ask themselves why do all this work if nothing can come of it anyway, I would say the longest journey begins but with a single step. So does our access to the countryside. And knowing where you want to walk is of great importance if you want to lobby your MP and your Rights of Way Department to do something about it. At the very least, agreements for permissive rights along field edge (or headland) paths could then be negotiated by DEFRA for an agreed minimum rental period. Choosing existing field margins and gates would of course help in bringing this about.

Another consideration illustrating the restrictions of the existing network in Sparsholt is the point that, although we live in a country parish, the village school children can only reach the local woods after traversing over a mile of footpath, lane and bridleway, and would have to return along the same route, in order to avoid having to walk along a stretch of narrow road carrying a lot of traffic at peak times.

7.2 Proposing new Rights of Way

I have attempted to establish some historical basis for the unanimous opposition of the private landowners, and even some of the public landowners, to any extension of the existing rights-of-way network. A rational analysis does not provide much in the way of support for this opposition, which is based on the premise that providing additional access would be similar to opening the floodgates. This argument is then contradicted by the claim that existing RoWs are anyway under-used, so why put landowners to all the trouble of instating new ones? And furthermore, the land is their factory for making food – how would factory owners like it if the public could walk through their factories any time they like?

This is of course akin to the argument how we would like it if any Tom, Dick and Harry could walk across our back garden. The answer was 'no problem if it was bigger than 100 hectares.' The factory comparison doesn't bear close scrutiny either. Factories are usually working all the year round, and any visitors would get in the way, quite apart from being exposed to the hazards of machinery or internal material movements, whereas the agricultural machinery used on the land is only in operation for at most two weeks of the year. When it comes to equipment theft, this is not likely to be instigated by walkers on footpaths.

So what about leaving gates open and letting dogs chase livestock? Modern technology should be able to cope with the former, and enforceable fines can cope with the latter. It is in any event time that gates across public rights of way are replaced by self-closing standardised gates designed to involve the minimum of installation and maintenance costs. Standardised gates? I can hear exclamations of horror from the traditionalists, perhaps from a similar background as those who were outraged when the post office installed standardised red telephone boxes around the country, and who are now equally outraged at the plans to remove these.

And how are we to deal with all the plastic rubbish left strewn along footpaths by the weekenders? Inexcusable, of course, but it's fair to mention that farmers are no laggards when it comes to leaving plastic bags scattered around fields wherever the wind moves them. Of course they have to use a lot of plastic in connection with their work, but they are no more entitled to let them drift across the countryside than the weekend walkers and picnickers.

Improving access in one's area should be of interest for readers with a similar bent of mind, even though many would regard this as a complete waste of time, on the basis that if the landowners are not willing to play, what is the point? There are in fact several points:

1. Being clear on where we want to go is a good start for any journey.

2. History is on our side. We have come a long way since the 1932 mass trespass at Kinder Scout.
3. The Government is committed to getting people on their feet, and I believe most of us support this aim.

As an interesting conjecture, I have tried to visualise the effect of the opening up of these new paths, inaugurated by some ceremony presided over by a local dignitary (probably not a landowner). Will this be followed by a stampede of the pent-up masses from Winchester and further afield? Not very likely. At most there might be a temporary initial swell due to the Winchester Ramblers' Association doing some inaugural celebratory walks. After that the usage will dwindle to an average of between two and ten walkers per day on any one new path, accompanied by an equivalent reduction in usage of the existing routes. This would certainly have a beneficial effect on the more popular long-distance routes which are subject to erosion due to excessive usage.

One additional consideration concerning walkers' access to the countryside is the provision of roadside parking in small lay-bys. This is of the utmost importance in facilitating and extending the available range of circular walking routes, and is of course of particular benefit to those coming from the nearby urban areas. My map of proposed new RoWs in Sparsholt therefore also includes proposed locations for these, which would extend the possibilities for circular walks considerably, both for parishioners and visitors from outside. Even then, at least some part of the resulting new circular walks would still entail walking along country lanes.

In this context I feel bound to mention the comment of

a land agent in an adjoining parish, who expressed surprise that the country lanes through his estate were not sufficient access to the countryside for ramblers. I can only assume that he never actually ventured out of his four-wheel drive to engage in this dangerous pursuit. He might soon have realised why walking along a winding lane excluded from longer views by impenetrable hedges is not a desirable form of relaxation. Apart from the lack of distant views, it involves having to be prepared to jump into the hedge, where this is possible, to avoid being mown down by another knight of the road testing his manhood by seeing how fast he could negotiate a blind bend.

Getting new Rights of Way established would come under the domain of the County Council, in our case Hampshire County Council Recreation and Heritage Department. In my own experience, they are timid in promoting new access to the countryside, on the basis that bribing landowners to agree to this would result in an unacceptable demand on their department's resources.

Let me illustrate the problem: some years ago, in my voluntary capacity of Sparsholt footpath scrutineer for the Winchester Ramblers' Association, I noticed that the fingerpost for one of the Parish footpaths was missing, and the route neither marked nor cleared for walkers. This path, it has to be said, was an anomaly created by the Government's policy in 1952 of letting parishes decide individually which footpaths they wanted to be put on what is now known as the 'definitive' map, without consultation with the adjoining parishes. In the event, Sparsholt decided to keep their part of the path in question open, whilst the adjoining parish decided to abandon theirs (the route of which, incidentally, got lost in the mists of intervening time). Result: we have a cul-de-sac.

As a result of my discovery that this cul-de-sac was missing, the landowner was requested to clear the path and the county erected another signpost carrying the message 'this is a cul-de-sac – please retrace your steps at the end.' To celebrate the re-instatement, I, together with other local ramblers walked it, with me feeling a bit like the grand old Duke of York, leading his troops up the hill to take in the extensive views from there, and then back down again. At least it wasn't a mass trespass (see illustration 18).

This, however, was not the end of the story, because shortly thereafter the landowner applied for the path to be closed because, in view of the fact that it didn't go anywhere, it was unlikely to attract any users. The Ramblers' Association's view, and that of the councillors at the meeting to adjudicate the matter, was 'better a cul-de-sac than nothing.' A factor influencing their decision was that the County RoW Department would be asked to take steps to re-establish the connecting path in the adjoining parish, once they were agreed where it went.

That was in the year 2000, and, not to my utter amazement, I should add, there have been no further developments. Still the cul-de-sac remains a footpath waiting to go some place, and unless something is done soon, that place will be oblivion. As already mentioned in the introduction, so did my attempt to re-establish a link across the adjacent parish on the basis that it went along the route of what was shown on the 1870 map as 'The Drove'. As an interim measure to obviate the possibility of oblivion, I have incorporated a proposal for a short link (6-7) with Forestry Commission land on my map.

Far from improving our local access network, recent years have seen a worsening of the situation. I refer in particular to the closure of an access into West Wood used by many locals for 20 years and more prior to its closure in 2000. This now means that access from Sparsholt village into an attractive part of Forestry land which is also part of the Farley Mount Country Park entails a deviation of a mile in total, and even this necessitates retracing ones steps over the same route for those wishing to return to their starting point. On my map I have also incorporated a proposed link (a part of 16-17) to alleviate this situation.

The Sparsholt College area also presents opportunities, though the farm manager's answer to the question of extending the existing right-of-way across the farm was negative. They already suffer from trespassers using the land for hare coursing, when they are not removing farm equipment under cover of darkness, although this may be mainly due to the fact that the existing footpath ends at a major road.

Creating a new link (4-5) on my map (to connect up with the bridleway to Farley Mount would cause few problems to either the College or the adjacent landowners, and at the same time establish another link to Clarendon Way long-distance path from Winchester. This could in fact be argued to represent a tourist attraction for walkers who are being canvassed to make use of Sparsholt College's holiday accommodation during the summer months. The provision of car parking (no. 5 on the map) would in addition open up the possibility of several additional circular walks in the area, some incorporating extensive views.

7.3 The wider scene

Scotland has had the freedom to roam across heathland and mountainside for centuries. On the continent, Sweden has the most civilised attitude to access. Their system, known as 'Allemansrat', permits public access to all land, the only proviso being that the landowner's personal privacy is not infringed. In Germany all woodland must be open to the public, subject to temporary restrictions during the culling season and the prohibition against the erection of tents other than on official campsites.

The Freedom to Roam Act (Countryside and Rights of Way, or CRoW Act 2000) applicable to England and Wales has been welcomed by walkers, but as already mentioned, it applies exclusively to land defined as being mountain, moor, heath and down, or registered commons. As it happens, apart from a very small common, none of these are present in Sparsholt or many other parishes across the country. As shown above, however, there is scope for numerous options for creating additional circular walks in the parish, and doubtlessly in most parishes in England and Wales.

Freedom to Roam does not encompass woodland, as it does in Germany, or river banks. With regard to the latter, I recall a correspondence with Hampshire County Council about the lack of riverside paths in the River Test valley. The Rights of Way Department were somewhat taken aback at my comments on this, having only just set up the 'Test Way' along a disused railway line for this purpose. Although no doubt better than nothing, I felt bound to point out that for much of its length it consists of a mainly dead straight tunnel of shrubbery with ne'er a view of the River Test except for the occasional

Rambler Eddie steps up search for missing link

A rambler is appealing for help in his search for a missing footpath.

Eddie Bush has already managed to persuade the authorities to re-open a neglected path near Sparsholt Corner, deep in

by David Banks

the countryside four miles west of Winchester. But he has literally run into a dead end...

The half-mile path now bears a unique sign—put up by the county council at his request, saying: "This footpath is a cul-de-sac–please return along the same route".

But Eddie is certainly not leaving it there...

He knows, from old maps, that there was another path called The Drove, which was closed 45 years ago and he is convinced that it once formed a continuation of the route into the neighbouring parish of Ashley.

Now he hopes to find someone who can remember it and so help him persuade the county council to reinstate the mile-long "missing link".

Eddie, a retired engineer and a keen member of Winchester Ramblers, has already applied for a map modification and he is hopeful that it will be heard soon.

"I'd be delighted to hear from anyone who knows about the history of this path between Ashley and Sparsholt, with a view to supplying evidence for the hearing," he said.

"In the meantime, we have to content ourselves with marching to the top of the hill to take in this view and then marching

them back down again. "Re-opening it would add significantly to the number of circular walks open to the people of Winchester without causing any serious hindrance to the cultivation of crops or preservation of game and other wildlife in the area."

His appeal to Hampshire County Council to create a network of circular routes for the Millennium was rejected earlier this year.

If you can help Eddie, he would be pleased to hear from you on 01962-776315 or e-mail invent@globalnet.co.uk.

• Welcome for right to roam page 25

On the road to nowhere...Eddie Bush and some of his fellow Winchester Ramblers survey their prospects of finding a missing footpath

18   No mass trespass

19a   Private Heritage : River Test – no access

19b   and trespassers

tantalising glimpse of it through gaps in the shrubbery, and virtually no distant views. I took the opportunity to put forward a number of footpath links which would alleviate this situation considerably, whereupon the Department suggested I might like to contact the landowners concerned and propose a dedication on their part, obviously banking on the fact that nobody in their right mind would undertake such a foolish enterprise.

They also failed to mention that DEFRA, although assisting riverside landowners through a scheme aimed at conserving the wetland habitat, known as the ESA (Environmentally Sensitive Areas scheme), is prevented through the Data Protection Act from letting on who these recipients of the public's beneficence are. We thus have the anomalous situation where, as taxpayers, we are subsidising landowners in helping them entertain wealthy business clients from abroad including an occasional American ex-president, together with those natives able to afford a fishing license along this part of the river, with not a chance of even getting near the river along its most attractive stretches. Not for us the chance to experience the uniquely peaceful riverside setting of the private stretches of the Test with glimpses of Lutyens' white chalk manor on the distant hillside. Perhaps the fishermen have time to appreciate this, but I suspect that their attention is focussed on bagging trout instead.

On an occasion a year or two ago when I accidentally strayed on to the banks of the Test reserved for fishing, I was challenged by a fisherman (backed up, I should add, by his spouse reclining in a Mercedes parked on the riverbank not many yards away). I explained that my presence in the area was merely prompted by photographic zeal. He was not impressed by this and suggested that I leave by the shortest route possible (where have I heard this suggestion before?!). Little did I know, at the time, that I might just as easily have bumped into ex-president George (without the W) Bush with his personal Ghilly, not to mention his bodyguards who would undoubtedly have wrestled me to the ground before I could have said as much as 'Good Morning'.

Illustration 19a shows such a private section of the River Test reserved for fishing, which shows what the general public is not permitted to experience, and illustration 19b what might be seen as an idyllic childhood experience of a river. Who would prefer to jet-set their children to a crowded Mediterranean beach if they had this opportunity on their doorstep? Without wishing to expose the subjects on the picture to prosecution, I can vouchsafe that it shows a tributary of a well-known Hampshire trout stream. Would I crack and divulge its location under torture? Probably!

On the subject of riverbank access I feel bound to relate an experience of mine which I would advise any fishermen amongst the readership to skip, particularly if they suffer from high blood pressure. It concerns a footpath which actually crosses the River Test on an extensive footbridge at one point (needless to say not the Test Way, which does not approach the river for most of its route). I was standing on this footbridge with my companions on a lovely summer's day gazing downstream watching the trout jumping to catch midges, when we became aware of a young couple wading up the middle of the river towards us. In the course of an ensuing conversation, we established that they had come to walk along the river bank, but since there were no footpaths there they decided to walk up mid-stream instead.

All this does point to a revision of our current access situation with regard to rivers. Whilst recognising the size and power of the fishing lobby, the walking lobby is on the ascendant, and the time may well be ripe to look at coming to some compromise such as reserving at least one side of our rivers for public access.

It's not just fields, woods, rivers and views that are not accessible to us. Another aspect of access to the countryside that needs to be mentioned is where this entails access to heritage sites and country parks. With regard to the former, we have a case in point in the adjoining parish, with the remains of Merdon Castle (one of Henry de Blois' twelve castles around Winchester) in private grounds. Although at one time there was a possibility of public access being provided as a quid pro quo for planning consent for a golf course on the adjoining land, the owners at the time eventually abandoned this project. My suggestion that they might still like to dedicate the access without the golf course met with the puzzling response that the castle is preserved under the auspices of English Heritage, and that they considered it would be best preserved for the nation if it remained closed to the public. Illustration 20b shows that the remains of the castle are now completely overgrown, perhaps more so than in bygone times, as shown in illustration 20a.

My enquiry with English Heritage drew the reply that Merdon Castle is actually protected as a nationally important monument under the Ancient Monuments and Archaeological Areas Act 1979, and that public access would interfere with the game bird habitats on the site. Furthermore, the owners already permit annual scout camps, and it is in any event possible for 'genuinely' interested persons to view the site by making an application in writing to the owners beforehand.

The letter ended on the conspiratorial note that the writer was sure I appreciated how controversial the issue of free access to private land had become. This I did not, since in my view it had been so for centuries. Since English Heritage 'exists to protect and promote England's spectacular historic environment and ensure that its past is researched and understood', it is somewhat puzzling for whom they and the owners are preserving the site. We must assume they are thinking of the game birds and the boy scouts, and perhaps some new generation in the future who can be entrusted with their heritage. And no, I refused to join the boy scouts; I like to think that I remain young at heart, but there are limits!

Access to nature reserves could arguably have an adverse effect on wildlife, and restrictions are understandable. Of equal importance, however, should be the adverse effect on the human inhabitants of the nearby conurbations if their access to the local countryside were to be restricted. This was in fact suggested in a 'Supplementary Memorandum by the United Kingdom Environmental Law Association'[4], which contained a report on discussions by managers of country parks owned by Hampshire County Council, quoting Farley Mount Country Park as being one of two which provide 'fairly minimal facilities and represent areas close to urban settlements which were already under significant informal recreational pressure and for which the County Council took over management primarily to control that pressure rather than encourage greater use.'

Whilst not suggesting that the weekend refugees from the

20a   18th Century Merdon Castle: open to all?

20b   and 21st century : closed to all but boy scouts

adjacent conurbations may now become liable to culling in addition to the muntjac deer, this does highlight the fact that there is a demand for access to the countryside which is not met by our existing access network. The time has come to look at the question of providing more access to the countryside, including riverbanks, woodland and even field margins where appropriate, regardless of whether or not any of it happens to be in a 'Freedom to Roam' area.

The government has issued many pious directives to local authorities with a view to taking positive steps to improve public access to the countryside. I quote an extract from one of the most recent, the Countryside Rights of Way Act 2002 -Sections 60-62: 'Local Rights of Way are a significant part of our heritage and a major recreational resource', and 'Local Highway authorities should consider the adequacy of access to and within attractive areas of countryside which might currently have few rights of way .....' As is so often the case with these directives, they have had little effect 'on the ground,' as one might very appropriately put it. Simple visions and sweeping statements, though good for the adrenalin, usually get swamped in the quagmire of the detail of parliamentary debates and committees. When the tide of emotion recedes, little is left but the flotsam of disillusion.

In the course of the 70th anniversary celebrations of the Kinder Scout trespass in 2002 the current Duke of Devonshire welcomed the assembled walkers to his estate and apologised for the intransigence of his ancestors in keeping the townies off their grouse moors. We should be grateful for his generosity and grace in doing so. Or perhaps we are grateful simply because we still cling to the notion that land, whether acquired by inheritance or sheer hard graft, should be inviolate from those who want to walk on it. Should we indeed be grateful for being made a gift of something we should consider a right?

Without exception the landowners I spoke to in Sparsholt regarded public access to their land as a nuisance. Although most of them accepted existing rights of way with what might be described as bad grace, they were adamant about not wanting any more. As one of them pointed out, Hampshire has a lot of footpaths – why should we want more in Sparsholt? I have already attempted to answer this query. On the wider scene, why should we want more access nationwide? The answer to that has to do with numbers. Recent research has shown that there are, on average, 38 million of us in Britain who walk for exercise or recreation at least once a month. Even if only 10% of these would welcome an extension of the existing public rights of way, that still leaves 3.8 million, yet the total number of agricultural landowners is 190,000, i.e. one land owner for every twenty walkers wanting more access. This brings us inevitably to the tricky question of the whole principle of landownership. If 'the land' ultimately belongs to 'us', perhaps on the basis that we are next in line to 'the crown', how can we assert our right for improved access? Before even attempting to do so, we have to be clear just how we define improved access. It has to mean extending the existing network of definitive rights of way outside the freedom to roam areas, to incorporate coasts, riversides, woodland and headlands (i.e. field margins). To achieve these aims in the face of recalcitrant landowners there are only two methods open to us: the stick, or the carrot, or combination of the two. The stick will have to be new legislation, the carrot financial compensation.

One way to make this possible is based on the idea of regarding land as a taxable asset. Thus, as with other forms of wealth in a democratic society, we tax it. This has been advocated by the International Union for Land Taxation, which is the originator of a petition to amend the UN Universal Declaration of Human Rights. The ultimate aim of this particular movement is to replace all taxes by land taxes, based on the idea that land is the ultimate source of our wealth, whether we own one tenth of a hectare or 100,000.

The idea of shifting the tax base of business rates to land values has also surfaced on the political agenda of the Liberal Democrats under the heading of ALTER (Action for Land Taxation and Economic Reform), with an All-Party Group on land reform already holding meetings. Once the principle of land taxation is accepted, the question of tax incentives for landowners giving improved access can be dealt with.

Another approach would be for any new subsidies to landowners and/or farmers to be subject to the provision of minimal new access as defined above. Seen in the context of total subsidies to the farming community in Sparsholt of £66,000 per annum in 2006, it would not be totally unreasonable to make say 10% of this subject to the provision of the additional four miles of footpaths proposed above. This would work out at approximately £1 per metre of new footpath per annum. If the same percentage were applied nationwide, DEFRA and/or the local authorities would have £229 million to spend on improved access, with a pro rata extension of the footpath network by nearly 14,000 miles. This works out at approximately £10 per metre of footpath per annum, which many would regard as more than reasonable compensation for landowners.

7.4 Where we have our say

Improved public access to the land cannot be dealt with on a local basis since it entails new legislation which can only be enacted by parliament. Lobbying one's MP is therefore the only route available to the individual, unless he or she joins an organisation devoted to doing just that. One's MP is more likely to take up a banner already carried by some major organisation such as the Rambler's Association or the Open Spaces Society, and even then his enthusiasm may well be tempered by his party affiliation and/or the make-up of his constituents. A prime example has to be the foxhunting issue, where an MP representing a primarily rural constituency is unlikely to have taken up with the anti-hunting lobby.

The question of access to heritage in England would appear to be the domain of English Heritage. My encounter with this organisation with regard to Merdon Castle in the adjoining parish, however, indicates that they seem to be mainly concerned with preserving it without ruffling the feathers of its owners by making public access a prerequisite for funding. This, considering that English Heritage is paid for out of our taxes to the tune of around £125 million per annum, and in addition charges us for entry to their properties, is, as they say, a bit rich.

Some readers may be interested to know that if they believe they have certain routes for walkers in mind which they think have historical claims to become rights of way, there is a deadline of 2026 beyond which no more claims can be filed. Seventeen years may seem a long while, but I have to inform them that when it comes to footpath claims it's no more then the blinking of an eyelid. I should add that my own experience was that pursuing this method has disappointing results, and even where the historical evidence is overwhelming, the protagonist is faced with devoting endless hours of research to his task.

Part 8

In Conclusion

Sparsholt is owned by a great number and variety of people, but the bulk of it belongs to just a few large landowners, and what they do with their land is reflected nationwide. Every year brings a change in the crop distribution reflecting the growing world demand for wheat, barley and biofuel crops. In addition, the demands of the international community for reductions in CO_2 emissions and the use of renewable energy sources are slowly changing our landscape. We are also seeing unfamiliar crops such as opium poppies, which have only been grown significantly since about six years ago to meet the demands of the NHS for diamorphine, and more recently, short rotation coppiced willow for use as fuel in wood-burning power stations.

The principal regulatory body for landowners is DEFRA, which has extensive powers in administering the subsidies available to landowners by way of Common Agricultural Policy payments and other subsidies. Public landowners such as the Forestry Commission also have considerable powers in pursuing policies which are to some extent dictated by adherence to international agreements such as the Kyoto protocol.

What the smaller landowners do on their land is of greater local significance, as witnessed by institutions such as the parish council, the school, the church, the village hall, the shop and post office, and the pubs. All are of great social importance, and when it comes to public institutions, they ultimately become effective due to a small minority who freely give of their time and energies to promote public welfare.

What happens on the land in Sparsholt is to some extent governed by the global situation. We are constrained by considerations of global warming and the worldwide harvests. Just as the country as a whole has to face up to its global responsibilities as regards global warming and biodiversity, the inhabitants of Sparsholt cannot live in isolation and ignore the needs for recreational access to the countryside from our nearby conurbations. In order to live up to our wider social responsibilities, we should make visitors from outside welcome by providing car parking and improved countryside access in our parish. This again should be reflected nationwide, and can only be brought about by legislation.

Whilst my proposals may seem utopian, there will come a day when we will look back and say in wonder, 'Can you believe there was a time when people weren't allowed to walk here?' In the existing situation it is important for campaigners to be clear where they want access. The rest will follow, even though it might take a while. The motto should be: 'Walkers of Britain unite – you have nothing to lose but your barbed wire!' In the words of David Miliband, our (then) Secretary of State for the Environment, at an anniversary celebration commemorating the mass trespass on Kinder Scout, 'Land, even private land, is a public good and we should assert our right to enjoy it. It should be accessible to all.' I drink to that!

Edmund Bush
Sparsholt, February 2009

References

Foreword
1 The free Dictionary – Google : http://legal-dictionary. thefreedictionary.com/land

Introduction
1 Winchester City Council – www.winchester.gov.uk/faqs

Part 1
1 Cahill, Kevin *Who owns Britain* (Edinburgh: Canongate Books 2001) p 52
2 Frantzen and Moffat *The Work of Work: Servitude, Slavery, and Labour in Medieval England* (Glasgow, Cruithne Press 1994) Chapter 'The End of Medieval Slavery'
3 as 1 p131-3
4 DEFRA Core Tables, Chapter 9, 2007-08 plans
5 HM Treasury Public Expenditure Statistical Analysis 2007
6 NHS web page
7 www.defra.gov.uk.environment/statistics/land

Part 2
1 Natural England, Reading (Hampshire Downs Team)
2 Report in Evening Standard by Anthony Hilton, Feb.2009
3 *Farmers Weekly Interactive* – Annual Farm Profits Survey (Jan 08)

Part 3
1 as 1(1) above p140
2 The Week 1 July 2006 *The Rise and Fall of Britain's industrialised forest*
3 Forestry Commission Annual Accounts 2006/07

4   Forestry Commission Great Britain and England Annual reports 2003/4
5   DEFRA news release 19.02.04 : *Achieving sustainable management of wild deer*

Part 4
1   Agriculture in the United Kingdom 2006
2   2006 UN Food and Agricultural Organisation report *Livestock's Long Shadow*
3   Friends of the Earth publication *Earthmatters Spring 2008* p.27
4   House of Commons News Release 19.2.07
5   DEFRA *Economics and Statistics – Indicator B6: Farm Income*

Part 5
1   Statistics of Education, Schools in England 2000

Part 6
1   Knowles, Cecilia *Sparsholt and Lainston*   (Chichester, Phillimore & Co. Ltd. 1981)

Part 7
1   DETR Press Office June 2000
2   As 1(1) p.9
3   Hampshire County Council – Hampshire Papers: *Hampshire and Australia*
4   UK Parliament Select Committee on Environment, Transport and Regional Affairs – *Supplementary Memorandum TCP 26 a (April 1999)*